Animals & People

A Selection of Essays
from Orion Magazine

Orion Readers are published by *Orion* magazine.
All essays appeared in *Orion*.

Orion
187 Main Street, Great Barrington, Massachusetts 01230
Telephone: 888/909-6568
Fax: 413/528-0676
www.orionmagazine.org

Design by Hans Teensma/Impress

Cover photograph by Jason Mintzer

This volume was made possible by generous support from the Summerlee Foundation and the Temple Family Private Foundation.

ISBN: 978-1-935713-10-4

In Memory of
Olivia Ladd Gilliam

CONTENTS

FOREWORD

THE RELATIONSHIP between humans and animals is complex. For some people, animals are simply "things" that can be owned, studied, killed, eaten. For others they are companions to be loved—though they may be "loved" in the wrong way, like the songbird in a cage, the little dog carried around, dressed in jacket and bows. For still others, animals are a way to reconnect with nature, a doorway to our innermost animal selves. *Animals & People*, like Pattiann Rogers's haunting and disturbing title poem, explores the whole contradictory, tragic, joyous, brutal, loving, and often puzzling nature of these relationships.

Attitudes to animals vary depending on the culture—children are brought up to love bull fighting or hate it, to stroke a dog or throw stones at it. The early naturalists whose books I read as a child were typically and unashamedly anthropomorphic. But then scientists and philosophers became obsessed with trying to prove that there was a real difference between ourselves and animals. In 1960 I began my long-term study of chimpanzees, the animal biologically and behaviorally most like us. Professors at Cambridge University subsequently told me I should have given the chimpanzees numbers rather than names, and that only human beings had personalities, minds, and emotions. But I had learned that this was not true from the teacher I had as a child—my dog, Rusty!

As more scientists began studying animals in the wild, and describing the complex social behavior of elephants, lions, baboons, and so on, it became ever clearer that the differences between "them" and "us" were of degree only. So today scientists are studying the mind and emotions not only of mammals, but birds and even octopuses. In her essay "Deep Intellect," Sy Montgomery has written enchantingly about the strange and secret world of the octopus, describing her relationship with one special individual, Athena.

It is because of these studies of the minds and emotions of animals—proving we are not the only creatures that can experience happiness, depression, and grief, nor the only ones capable of psychological as well as physical suffering—that we can understand the full horror of human cruelty to animals. But one of the many things I love about this book is that none of the authors are militant. Lisa Couturier could so easily have ranted against the horrific treatment of horses in the slaughterhouses. We would not blame her. Instead she describes what happens objectively, but so vividly that we feel the terror and agony as though we too were there. The images conjured up by her words have joined countless others of the suffering of the billions of animals raised in factory farms, suffering that ends only after death. Just because an animal is raised for meat does this mean it has no life force, no feelings, no ability to suffer pain, to know fear?

Working against such presumptions are the many essays in this book in which the authors express a sense of wonder. Kathleen Jamie marvels at the fantastic ocean journeys of the minute storm petrel. Indeed, migrations are one of the wonders of nature, whether we think of birds, butterflies, fishes, whales, or the great herds of wildebeests and caribou. Amy Leach imagines the life of the giant panda. Her essay is full of humor, poking gentle fun at this strange bear who, to his own detriment, must confine himself to a diet of bamboo. David Gessner falls in love with pelicans, their prehistoric lineage, their graceful flight, their "Buddha-like calm." They help him reconnect with the natural world, something he knows is necessary for his well-being. And Brian Doyle is utterly fascinated by sturgeons, those truly remarkable giant fishes. I have long wanted to see them, and reading Doyle's words is the next best thing. I especially loved meeting one very special, very old male called Herman.

J. B. MacKinnon is fascinated by the elderly individuals of the animal world, describing how knowledge gained during a long life can be vital to the well-being of the group. Only old elephants can remember the whereabouts of a water hole, visited during a drought in their youth. But old age has its drawbacks (as I, approaching my eightieth year, know only too well!). Very old elephants can only eat softer foods as their last molar becomes increasingly worn. I have seen the teeth of very old chimpanzees and baboons that are worn down to the gums. MacKinnon also writes of the cross-species friendships sometimes developed by old animals. And by old humans too.

There is also much poetry in this book, and not only in the haunting opening words of Pattiann Rogers. There is poetry in the elegy of Mary Oliver as she mourns the passing of a place that she loved and, in doing so, confers on it immortality not only in the libraries of the future but also in our hearts.

Two essays discuss the problems that arise as our human populations grow and more and more wilderness areas are "developed." Shrinking habitats force wild animals ever closer to our homes, even into our cities. In "New Dog in Town," Christopher Ketcham writes about the urban coyotes, their intelligence and resilience. I love his sense of humor as he describes individuals who have made their homes in city parks and golf courses.

I once watched a female coyote who wanted to follow her mate across a road. Five times she took a few steps forward, then retreated, then finally gave up. Too bad deer are not so cautious. As they wander into urban gardens, so many are hit by cars, especially at night. Craig Childs describes the one occasion when he could not avoid such an accident. He writes with such poignancy that my eyes filled with tears as I read. I shall be forever haunted by his essay, the poetry of his words. And it is clear that he will be too.

We must be grateful to *Orion* for orchestrating this book. There is much to learn here from those who truly care about the animals with whom we share, or should share, our planet. People who are at the edge of a deep understanding. People who marvel at the life force of these other beings. People who mourn the harm that we inflict on their innocence, thus damaging ourselves.

JANE GOODALL, PhD, DBE
Founder, the Jane Goodall Institute &
UN Messenger of Peace
www.janegoodall.org

Animals & People

PATTIANN ROGERS

ANIMALS AND PEOPLE

The human heart in conflict with itself

Some of us like to photograph them. Some
of us like to paint pictures of them. Some of us
like to sculpt them and make statues and carvings
of them. Some of us like to compose music
about them and sing about them. And some of us
like to write about them.

Some of us like to go out
and catch them and kill them and eat them. Some
of us like to hunt them and shoot them and eat them.
Some of us like to raise them, care for them and eat
them. Some of us just like to eat them.

And some of us
name them and name their seasons and name their hours,
and some of us, in our curiosity, open them up
and study them with our tools and name their parts.
We capture them, mark them and release them,
and then we track them and spy on them and enter
their lives and affect their lives and abandon
their lives. We breed them and manipulate them
and alter them. Some of us experiment
upon them.

We put them on tethers and leashes,
in shackles and harnesses, in cages and boxes,
inside fences and walls. We put them in yokes
and muzzles. We want them to carry us and pull us
and haul for us.

And we want some of them
to be our companions, some of them to ride on our fingers
and some to ride sitting on our wrists or on our shoulders
and some to ride in our arms, ride clutching our necks.
We want them to walk at our heels.

We want them to trust
us and come to us, take our offerings, eat from our hands.
We want to participate in their beauty. We want to assume
their beauty and so possess them. We want to be kind
to them and so possess them with our kindness and so
partake of their beauty in that way.

And we want them
to learn our language. We try to teach them our language.
We speak to them. We put *our* words in *their* mouths.
We want *them* to speak. We want to know what they see
when they look at us.

We use their heads and their bladders
for balls, their guts and their hides and their bones
to make music. We skin them and wear them for coats,
their scalps for hats. We rob them, their milk
and their honey, their feathers and their eggs.
We make money from them.

We construct icons of them.
We make images of them and put their images on our clothes
and on our necklaces and rings and on our walls
and in our religious places. We preserve their dead
bodies and parts of their dead bodies and display
them in our homes and buildings.

We name mountains
and rivers and cities and streets and organizations
and gangs and causes after them. We name years and time
and constellations of stars after them. We make mascots
of them, naming our athletic teams after them. Sometimes
we name ourselves after them.

We make toys of them
and rhymes of them for our children. We mold them
and shape them and distort them to fit our myths
and our stories and our dramas. We like to dress up
like them and masquerade as them. We like to imitate them
and try to move as they move and make the sounds they make,
hoping, by these means, to enter and become the black
mysteries of their being.

Sometimes we dress them
in our clothes and teach them tricks and laugh at them
and marvel at them. And we make parades of them
and festivals of them. We want them to entertain us
and amaze us and frighten us and reassure us
and calm us and rescue us from boredom.

We pit them
against one another and watch them fight one another,
and we gamble on them. We want to compete with them

ourselves, challenging them, testing our wits and talents
against their wits and talents, in forests and on plains,
in the ring. We want to be able to run like them and leap
like them and swim like them and fly like them and fight
like them and endure like them.

We want their total
absorption in the moment. We want their unwavering devotion
to life. We want their oblivion.

Some of us give thanks
and bless those we kill and eat, and ask for pardon,
and this is beautiful as long as they are the ones dying
and we are the ones eating.

And as long as we are not
seriously threatened, as long as we and our children
aren't hungry and aren't cold, we say, with a certain
degree of superiority, that we are no better
than any of them, that any of them deserve to live
just as much as we do.

And after we have proclaimed
this thought, and by so doing subtly pointed out
that we are allowing them to live, we direct them
and manage them and herd them and train them and follow
them and map them and collect them and make specimens
of them and butcher them and move them here and move
them there and we place them on lists and we take
them off of lists and we stare at them and stare
at them and stare at them.

We track them in our sleep.
They become the form of our sleep. We dream of them.
We seek them with accusation. We seek them
with supplication.

And in the ultimate imposition,
as Thoreau said, we make them bear the burden
of our thoughts. We make them carry the burden
of our metaphors and the burden of our desires and our guilt
and carry the equal burden of our curiosity and concern.
We make them bear our sins and our prayers and our hopes
into the desert, into the sky, into the stars.
We say we kill them for God.

We adore them and we curse
them. We caress them and we ravish them. We want them
to acknowledge us and be with us. We want them to disappear
and be autonomous. We abhor their viciousness and lack
of pity, as we abhor our own viciousness and lack of pity.
We love them and we reproach them, just as we love
and reproach ourselves.

We will never, we cannot,
leave them alone, even the tiniest one, ever, because we know
we are one with them. Their blood is our blood. Their breath
is our breath, their beginning our beginning, their fate
our fate.

Thus we deny them. Thus we yearn
for them. They are among us and within us and of us,
inextricably woven with the form and manner of our being,
with our understanding and our imaginations.
They are the grit and the salt and the lullaby
of our language.

We have a need to believe they are there,
and always will be, whether we witness them or not.
We need to know they are there, a vigorous life maintaining
itself without our presence, without our assistance,
without our attention. We need to know, we *must* know,
that we come from such stock so continuously and tenaciously
and religiously devoted to life.

We know we are one with them,
and we are frantic to understand how to actualize that union.
We attempt to actualize that union in our many stumbling,
ignorant and destructive ways, in our many confused
and noble and praiseworthy ways.

For how can we possess dignity
if we allow them no dignity? Who will recognize our beauty
if we do not revel in their beauty? How can we hope
to receive honor if we give no honor? How can we believe
in grace if we cannot bestow grace?

We want what we cannot
have. We want to give life at the same moment
we are taking it, nurture life at the same moment we light
the fire and raise the knife. We want to live, to provide,
and not be instruments of destruction, instruments
of death. We want to reconcile our "egoistic concerns"
with our "universal compassion." We want the lion
and the lamb to be one, the lion and the lamb *within*
finally to dwell together, to lie down together
in peace and praise at last.

(1997)

DAVID GESSNER

LEARNING TO SURF

Because stability just might be overrated

OUT JUST BEYOND the breaking waves they sit there bobbing, two groups of animals, avian and human, pelicans and surfers. As they rise and fall on humps of water, the pelicans look entirely unperturbed, their foot-long bills pulled like blades into scabbards, fitting like puzzle pieces into the curves of their throats. The surfers, mostly kids, look equally casual. A girl lies supine on her board, looking up at the sky, one leg crossed over the other in an almost exaggerated posture of relaxation. For the most part the birds and surfers ignore each other, rising up and dropping down together as the whole ocean heaves and then sighs.

Pelicans are particularly buoyant birds and they bob high on the water as the surfers paddle and shift in anticipation. There is no mistaking that this is the relatively tense calm of *before*, rest before exertion. Soon the waves pick up and the kids paddle furiously, gaining enough speed to pop up and ride the crests of breaking surf. They glide in toward the beach where I stand, the better ones carving the water and ducking under and cutting back up through the waves.

I just recently moved to this southern island town, but I

have been here long enough to know that those who pursue this sport are guided by a kind of laid-back monomania. Each morning I bring my four-month-old daughter down to the local coffee shop, and each morning the talk is of one thing. The ocean, I've learned, is always referred to as it.

"What did it look like this morning?" one surfer asked another a few mornings back.

"Sloppy."

Remembering my own early-morning glance at the water I could understand what he meant, the way a series of waves came from the northwest, while another group muscled up from the south, and how the two collided and kicked up. Aesthetically it was beautiful, but practically, at least from a surfer's point of view, it made for a landscape of chop—not much to get excited about.

Another morning I heard this:

"How does it look today, dude?"

"Small."

"Nothing?"

"You can go out there if you want to build your morale."

It's easy enough to laugh at these kids, but I like the physical nature of their obsession, the way their lives center on being strong animals. In *When Elephants Weep*, Jeffrey Masson speculates that animals feel *funktionslust*, a German word meaning "pleasure taken in what one can do best." The strongest of the surfers, the ones who have grown up on the waves, must certainly feel this animal pleasure as they glide over and weave through the water.

I watch the surfers for a while longer, but when the pelicans lift off, I turn my focus toward their even more impressive athletic feats. Pelicans are huge and heavy birds, and the initial liftoff, as they turn into the wind and flap hard, is awkward. But once in the air they are all grace. They pull in

their feet like landing gear and glide low between the troughs
of the waves, then lift up to look for fish, flapping several
times before coasting. If you watch them enough, a rhythm
reveals itself: effort, *glide*, effort, *glide*. They are looking for
small fish—menhaden or mullet most likely—and when they
find what they are searching for they gauge the depth of the
fish, and therefore the necessary height of the dive, a gauging
guided by both instinct and experience. Then they pause, lift,
measure again, and finally, plunge. The birds bank and twist
and plummet, following their divining-rod bills toward the
water. A few of them even turn in the air in a way that gives
the impression they are showing off. If they were awkward in
takeoff, now they are glorious.

There is something symphonic about the way the group hits
the water, one bird after another: *thwuck, thwuck, thwuck.* At the
last second before contact they become feathery arrows, thrust-
ing their legs and wings backward and flattening their gular
pouches. They are not tidy like terns and show no concern for
the Olympian aesthetics of a small splash, hitting the surface
with what looks like something close to recklessness. As soon
as they strike the water, instinct triggers the opening of the
huge pouch, and it umbrellas out, usually capturing fish, plural.
While still underwater they turn again, often 180 degrees, so
that when they emerge they'll be facing into the wind for takeoff

And when they pop back up barely a second later, they
almost instantly assume a sitting posture on the water, once
again bobbing peacefully. It's a little like watching a man serve
a tennis ball who then, after the follow-through, hops immediately into a La-Z-Boy.

The pelicans calm me, which is good. I have tried to maintain
a relaxed attitude since moving to this island, but at times it's
hard. I had vowed that I would stay forever on Cape Cod, my

old home, but it was my writing about how much I loved the Cape that led to the offer of a teaching job in this overcrowded North Carolina resort town of outboard motors, condos, and southern accents. My wife, Nina, had just given birth to our daughter, Hadley, and the lure of health insurance and a steady paycheck was irresistible.

The truth is, the move has unsettled me: in coming to this new place I find myself, and my confidence, getting shaky. If I've behaved well publicly, in the privacy of our new apartment I've at times started to fall apart. As each day unfolds, I grow ever less sure of myself.

One of the things that disorients me is the heat. It's the kind of heat that makes you want to lie down and give up, to start to cry and throw out your arms in surrender. I've known brutal cold in my life, but cold has the advantage of invigoration, at least initially. Now I understand the logic behind siestas; every instinct tells you to crawl to a cool, dank place and lie there and be still.

Lifting my daughter into our un-air-conditioned Honda Civic feels like sliding her into a kiln, so we are desperately trying to buy a new car. But today the Toyota guy calls with bad news. Our credit report has come back and our loan has been rejected.

"You have weak stability," he tells me, reading from the report.

I nod and consider the poetry of his words.

But there are other moments, moments when I sense that this may not be such a bad place to live. With summer ending, the parking lots have begun to empty. There are fewer beach walkers and more pelicans. Each morning I take long walks with Hadley, and have begun to take field notes on my daughter. I'm struck daily by her creatureliness, and the fact that this squirming little apelike animal, barely two feet high, has somehow been allowed to live in the same house with us. Nothing cuts through my doubts about having moved here quite like this new ritual of walking with my daughter in a papooselike contraption on my chest. On good days we make it all the way to the south end of the island where we stare out at the channel.

Many things have caught me off guard about being a father, but the most startling thing has been the sheer animal pleasure. "Joy is the symptom by which right conduct is measured," wrote Joseph Wood Krutch of Thoreau. If that's true then my conduct these days must be excellent.

This morning we watch two immature, first-year pelicans fly right over the waves, belly to belly with their shadows. It's exhilarating the way they lift up together and sink down again, rollercoastering, their wings nicking the crests of the waves. Eight more adult birds skim right through the valley between the waves, gliding by the surfers, sweeping upward before plopping onto the water.

Feeling that it's only polite to get to know my new neighbors, I've begun to read about the birds. I've learned that the reason they fly through the troughs between the waves is to cut down on wind resistance, which means they, like the surfers they fly past, are unintentional physicists. When I first started watching pelicans I kept waiting to hear their calls, expecting a kind of loud *quack-quork*, like a cross between a raven and a duck. But my books confirm what I have already noticed, that adult pelicans go through their lives as near mutes. Whether perched atop a piling in classic silhouette or crossing bills with a mate or bobbing in the surf, they remain silent.

Another group of adult birds heads out to the west, toward the channel, as Hadley and I turn home. Before moving here I never knew that pelicans flew in formations. They are

not quite as orderly as geese—their Vs always slightly out
of whack—and the sight of them is strange and startling to
someone from the North. Each individual takes a turn at the
head of the V, since the lead bird exerts the most effort and
energy while the birds that follow draft the leader like bike
racers. These platoons fly overhead at all hours of day, ap-
pearing so obviously prehistoric that it seems odd to me that
people barely glance up, like ignoring a fleet of pterodactyls.

Yesterday I saw a bird point its great bill at the sky and
then open its mouth until it seemed to almost invert its
pouch. My reading informs me that these exercises are common, a way to stretch out the distensible gular pouch so that
it maintains elasticity. Even more impressive, I learn that the
pouch, when filled, can hold up to twenty-one pints—seven-
teen and a half pounds—of water.

"I have had a lifelong love affair with terns," wrote my
friend from Cape Cod, John Hay, a writer whom I have always
admired for his sense of rootedness. I've come to pelicans late
and so can't have my own lifelong affair. But I am developing
something of a crush.

I'm not a good watcher. Well, that's not exactly true. I'm a
pretty good watcher. It's just that sooner or later I need to do
more than watch. So today I am floating awkwardly on my
neighbor Matt's surfboard, paddling with my legs in a frantic
eggbeater motion, attempting this new sport in this new place
while keeping one eye on the pelicans. Even though you can't
bring your binoculars, it turns out that this is a great way to
birdwatch. The pelicans fly close to my board, and for the first
time I understand how enormous they are. I've read that they
are fifty inches from bill to toe, and have six-and-a-half-foot
wingspans, but these numbers don't convey the heft of their
presence. One bird lands next to me and sits on the water,

tucking its ancient bill into its throat. Up close its layered feathers look very unfeatherlike, more like strips of petrified wood. I watch it bob effortlessly in the choppy ocean. Most birds with webbed feet have three toes, but brown pelicans have four, and their webbing is especially thick. While this makes for awkward waddling on land, it also accounts for how comfortable the birds look in the water.

I'm not nearly as comfortable. Two days ago I spent an hour out here with Matt, and yesterday we came out again. Despite his patience and coaching, I never stood up on my board, in fact I never made more than the most spastic attempts. Today has been no better. The best things about surfing so far are watching the birds and the way my body feels afterward when I am scalding myself in our outdoor shower. So it is with some surprise that I find myself staring back with anticipation as a series of good waves roll in, and it is with something close to shock that I find myself suddenly, mysteriously, riding on top of that one perfect (in my case, very small) wave. Before I have time to think I realize that I am standing, actually standing up and surfing. The next second I am thrown into the waves and smashed about.

But that is enough to get a taste for it.

I have now been practicing my new art for three days. The pelicans have been practicing theirs for 30 million years. It turns out that the reason they look prehistoric is simple: they are. Fossils indicate that something very close to the same bird we see today was among the very first birds to take flight. They were performing their rituals—diving, feeding, courting, mating, nesting—while the world froze and thawed, froze and thawed again, and while man, adaptable and relatively frenetic, came down from the trees and started messing with fire and farming and guns.

What struck me first about these curious-looking birds was the grace of their flight. Not so the early ornithologists. In 1922, Arthur Cleveland Bent wrote of their "grotesque and quiet dignity" and called them "silent, dignified and stupid birds." A contemporary of Bent's, Stanley Clisby Arthur, went even further, describing the pelicans' habits with something close to ridicule. Arthur writes of the pelicans' "lugubrious expressions" and "ponderous, elephantine tread" and "undemonstrative habits," and says of their mating rituals that "they are more befitting the solemnity of a funeral than the joyous display attending most nuptials." His final insult is calling their precious eggs "a lusterless white."

Even modern writers seem to feel the need to lay it on thick: as I read I make a list of words that includes "gawky," "awkward," "comical," "solemn," "reserved," and, simply, "ugly." It never occurred to me that pelicans were so preposterous, though I'll admit that recently, as I kayaked by a sandbar full of birds, I laughed while watching a pelican waddle though a crowd of terns, like Gulliver among the Lilliputians. But "ugly" seems just mean-spirited.

When not seeing pelicans as comic or grotesque, human beings often describe them as sedate and sagelike. Perhaps this springs from a dormant human need to see in animals the qualities we wish we had. Compared to our own harried, erratic lives, the lives of the pelicans appear consistent, reliable, even ritualistic, as befits a bird that has been doing what it's been doing for thirty million years. And compared to their deep, consistent lives, my own feels constantly reinvented, improvised. But before I get too down on myself, I need to remember that that's the kind of animal I am, built for change, for adaptation. Long before we became dull practitioners of agriculture, human beings were nomads, wanderers, capable of surviving in dozens of different environments.

Though barely able to hold their heads up at birth and fed regurgitated food by their parents while in the nest, newborn pelicans fledge within three months. The one-year-olds I watch flying overhead are already almost as capable as their parents, while my daughter will need our help and guidance for many years to come. But this too makes evolutionary sense: one reason for our long infancy and childhood is to give the human mind time to adapt creatively to thousands of different circumstances. Pelicans, on the other hand, are ruled by a few simple laws and behaviors. Still, at the risk of romanticizing, I like the sense of calm the birds exude, the sense of timelessness, of ritual and grace.

We humans face a different set of problems. Our bodies still run on rhythms we only half understand (and often ignore), and we have adapted ourselves beyond ritual. To a certain extent all rules are off. The life of a hunter or farmer, the life that all humans lived until recently, directly connected us to the worlds of animals and plants, and to the cycles of the seasons. Without these primal guidelines, we are left facing a kind of uncertainty that on good days offers a multifarious delight of options, and on bad days offers chaos. Ungrounded in this new place, I am acutely sensitive to both possibilities. And while it isn't comfortable building a foundation on uncertainty, it has the advantage of being consistent with reality. Maybe in this world the best we can do is to not make false claims for certainty, and try to ride as gracefully as we can on the uncertain.

The human brain is no match for depression, for the chaos of uprootedness. To try to turn our brains on ourselves, to think we can solve our own problems within ourselves, is to get lost in a hall of mirrors. But there is a world beyond the human world and that is a reason for hope. From a very selfish human perspective, we need more than the human.

Water and birds have always helped me live, have always lifted me beyond myself, and this morning I paddle out beyond the breakers and lie with my back to the surfboard just like the girl I saw in early fall. But while my legs may be crossed casually, I spend most of the time worrying about falling off. Even so, as I bob up and down on the waves, the whole ocean lifting and dropping below me, my niggling mind does quiet for a minute. And then it goes beyond quiet. I'm thinking of Hadley, sitting up now and holding her own bottle, and I feel my chest fill with the joy these small achievements bring. She will be a strong girl I suspect, an athlete. And, no doubt, if we stay here she will become a surfer, delighting in her own funktionslust.

Glancing up at the pelicans flying overhead, I notice that there is something slightly backward-leaning about their posture, particularly when they are searching for fish, as if they were peering over spectacles. From directly below they look like giant kingfishers. But when they pull in their wings they change entirely: a prehistoric Bat Signal shining over Gotham. Then I see one bird with tattered feathers whose feet splay out crazily before he tucks to dive. When he tucks, dignity is regained, and the bird shoots into the water like a spear.

Inspired by that bird, I decide to turn my attention back to surfing. I catch a few waves, but catch them late, and so keep popping wheelies and being thrown off the surfboard. Then, after a while, I remember Matt telling me that I've been putting my weight too far back on the board. So on the next wave, almost without thinking, I shift my weight forward and pop right up. What surprises me most is how easy it is. I had allotted months for this advancement, but here I am, flying in toward the beach on top of a wave, its energy surging below. A wild giddiness fills me. It's cliché to say that I am completely in the present moment as this happens, and it's also not really true. Halfway to shore I'm already imagining telling Nina about my great success, and near the end of my ride, as the great wave deposits me in knee-deep water, I find myself singing the *Hawaii Five-O* theme song right out loud.

Though no one is around I let out a little hoot, and by the time I jump off the board I'm laughing out loud. A week ago I watched some kids, who couldn't have been older than twelve or thirteen, as they ran down the beach on a Friday afternoon. Happy that school was out, they sprinted into the water before diving onto their boards and gliding into the froth of surf. I'm not sprinting, but I do turn around and walk the surfboard back out until I am hip deep, momentarily happy to be the animal I am, my whole self buzzing from a ride that has been more the result of grace than effort. Then, still laughing a little, I climb on top of the board and paddle back into the waves.

I could end on that note of grace, but it wouldn't be entirely accurate. The year doesn't conclude triumphantly with me astride the board, trumpets blaring, as I ride that great wave to shore. Instead it moves forward in the quotidian way years do, extending deep into winter and then once again opening up into spring. As the days pass, my new place becomes less new, and the sight of the squadrons of pelicans loses some of its thrill. This too is perfectly natural, a process known in biology as habituation. Among both birds and humans, habituation is, according to my books, the "gradual reduction in the strength of a response due to repetitive stimulation." This is a fancy way of saying we get used to things.

While the pelican brain repeats ancient patterns, the human brain feeds on the new. On a biological level novelty is vital to the human experience: at birth the human brain is wired so that it is attracted to the unfamiliar. I see this in my daughter as she begins to conduct more sophisticated experi-

ments in the physical world. True, all of these experiments
end the same way, with her putting the object of experimen-
tation into her mouth, but soon enough she will move on
to more sophisticated interactions with her environment.
She's already beginning to attempt language and locomotion.
Although pelicans her age are already diving for fish, she, as a
Homo sapiens, can afford to spot *Pelecanus occidentalis* a lead.
She will gain ground later. Her long primate infancy will allow
her relatively enormous brain to develop in ways that are as
foreign to the birds as their simplicity is to us, and will allow
that brain to fly to places the birds can never reach.

While I acknowledge these vast differences between bird
and human, there is something fundamentally unifying in
the two experiences of watching the pelicans and watching
my daughter. There is a sense that both experiences help me
fulfill Emerson's still-vital dictum: "First, be a good animal."
For me fatherhood has intensified the possibility of loss, the
sense that we live in a world of weak stability. But it has also
given me a more direct connection to my animal self, and so,
in the face of the world's chaos, I try to be a good animal. I get
out on the water in an attempt to live closer to what the nature
writer Henry Beston called "an elemental life."

I keep surfing into late fall, actually getting up a few
times. But then one day I abruptly quit. On that day it is big,
much too big for a beginner like me. I should understand
this when I have trouble paddling out, the waves looming
above me before throwing my board and self backward. And
I should understand this as I wait to catch waves, the watery
world lifting me higher than ever before. But despite the quiet
voice that is telling me to go home I give it a try, and before
I know it I am racing forward, triumphant and exhilarated,
until the tip of my board dips under and the wave bullies into
me from behind and I am thrown, rag-doll style, and held

under by the wave. Then I'm tossed forward again and the board, tethered to my foot by a safety strap, recoils and slams into my head. I do not black out; I emerge and stagger to the shore, touching my hand to the blood and sand on my face. The next night I teach my Forms of Creative Nonfiction class with a black eye.

So that is enough, you see. One of the new territories I am entering is that of middle age, and the world doesn't need too many middle-aged surfers.

I feared fatherhood, but most of the results of procreation have been delightful ones. One exception, however, is the way that disaster seems to loom around every corner—disaster that might befall my daughter, my wife, myself. No sense adding "death by surfing" to the list.

While I have naturally begun to take the pelicans for granted, they still provide daily pleasures throughout the winter. What I lose in novelty, I gain in the early stages of intimacy. I see them everywhere: as I commute to work they fly low in front of my windshield; they placidly perch atop the pilings while I sip my evening beer on the dock near our house; they bank above me as I drive over the drawbridge to town. My research reveals that in March they begin their annual ritual of mating: a male offers the female a twig for nest-building and then, if she accepts, they bow to each other before embarking on the less elegant aspect of the ritual, the actual mating, which lasts no more than twenty seconds. These rituals are taking place, as they should, in privacy, twenty miles south on a tiny island in the mouth of the Cape Fear River. The eggs are laid in late March or early April and a month-long period of incubation begins.

Around the midpoint of incubation, my human family achieves its own milestone. Throughout the spring I have continued to carry my daughter down the beach to watch the pelicans fish, but today is different from the other days. Today Hadley no longer rests in a pouch on my chest but walks beside me hand in hand.

I remind myself that the mushiness I feel at this moment, the sensation that some describe as sentimentality, also serves an evolutionary purpose. With that softening comes a fierceness, a fierce need to protect and aid and sacrifice. This is not a theoretical thing but a biological one. In fact this transformation borders the savage, and here too the pelicans have long served humans as myth and symbol. "I am like a pelican of the wilderness," reads Psalm 102. At some point early Christians got it into their heads that pelicans fed their young with the blood from their own breasts, a mistake perhaps based on the red at the tip of some pelican bills, or, less plausibly, on their habit of regurgitating their fishy meals for their young. Whatever the roots of this misapprehension, the birds became a symbol of both parental sacrifice and, on a grander scale, of Christ's own sacrifice. The images of pelicans as self-stabbing birds, turning on their own chests with their bills, were carved in stone and wood and still adorn churches all over Europe. Later, the parental symbol was sometimes reversed, so that Lear, railing against his famous ingrate offspring, calls them "those pelican daughters."

The year culminates in a single day, a day full of green, each tree and bird defined sharply as if with silver edges. I kiss Nina and Hadley goodbye while they are still asleep and head out at dawn to the road where Walker will pick me up. Walker Golder is the deputy director of the North Carolina Audubon Society, a friend of a new friend, and today he takes me in a small outboard down to the islands at the mouth of the Cape Fear River. We bomb through a man-made canal called Snow's Cut and I smile stupidly at the clarity of the colors: the blue water, the brown eroding banks, the green above.

We stop at four islands. The southernmost of these is filled with ibis nests—11,504 to be exact. Ten percent of North America's ibises begin their lives here, and at one point we stand amid a snowy blizzard of birds, vivid white plumage and flaming bills swirling around us. Next we visit an island of terns, the whole colony seemingly in an irritable mood. This island, and its nearby twin, were formed when the river was dredged in the '70s by the U.S. Army Corps of Engineers, which used the sand to consciously aid the Audubon Society in an attempt to create nesting grounds. Terns, like ibises and pelicans, require isolated breeding areas, preferably islands, and this human experiment, this marriage of birders and engineers, has worked to perfection. We watch as a pair of royal terns spiral above us in their courtship dance.

The terns are impressive, but the highlight of the day for me is North Pelican Island, the nesting ground of almost all of the pelicans I have watched over the last year. Hundreds of pelicans sit on their ground nests, some of which are as big as beanbag chairs. They watch impassively as we approach. The old naturalists might have called these birds "undemonstrative" and "lugubrious," but I'll go with "calm." In fact, while we're anthropomorphizing, I might as well put "Buddha-like" in front of calm. It's hard not to project this on them after experiencing the wild defensiveness of the tern colony. The pelicans barely glance up at us. Theirs is a much different survival strategy, a much quieter one, but natural for such a big bird with no native predators on these islands. I crunch up through the marsh elder and phragmites to a spot where two hundred or so pelicans are packed together, sitting on their nests, incubating. Some still have the rich chestnut patches on the backs of their heads and necks, a delightful chocolate brown: leftover breeding plumage. They sit in what I now rec-

ognize as their characteristic manner, swordlike bills tucked
into the fronts of their long necks.

While the birds remain quiet and calm, there is a sense
of urgency here. This marsh island, like most of the islands
that pelicans breed on, is very close to sea level. One moon-
tide storm could wash over it and drown the season out. It is
a time of year marked by both wild hope and wild precarious-
ness, danger and growth going hand in hand. The birds are
never more vulnerable, and as a father, I know the feeling.

I'm not sure exactly what I gain from intertwining my
own life with the lives of the animals I live near, but I enjoy
it on a purely physical level. Maybe I hope that some of this
calm, this sense of ritual, will be contagious. If the pelicans
look lugubrious to some, their effect on me is anything but.
And so I indulge myself for a moment and allow myself to
feel unity with the ancient birds. It may sound trite to say that
we are all brothers and sisters, all united, but it is also simply
and biologically true. DNA undermines the myth of our species' uniqueness, and you don't need a science degree to reach
this conclusion. We are animals, and when we pretend we are
something better, we become something worse.

Having seen these fragile nesting grounds a thousand
times before, Walker is to some extent habituated to them. He
is also more responsible than any other human being for their
protection. "We only visit briefly in the cool of the morning,"
he explains, "so not to disturb the birds." Playing tour guide,
he walks in closer to the nests and gestures for me to follow.
He points to some eggs that look anything but lusterless, and
then to another nest where we see two birds, each just a day
old. Though pelicans develop quickly, they are born feather-
less and blind, completely dependent on their parents, their
lives a wild gamble. Heat regulation, Walker explains, is a big
factor in nestling survival. Pelican parents must shade their

young on hot days, and one dog let loose on this island while the owner gets out of his boat to take a leak could drive the parents from the nest, resulting in the deaths of hundreds of nestlings.

But we are not thinking about death, not right now. We are instead watching these tiny purple dinosaurs that could fit in the palm of your hand, the beginnings of their extravagant bills already in embryonic evidence. And then, in a neighboring nest an egg trembles. There's a tapping, and a pipping out from within.

A small blind purple head emerges from the shell. "Something only a mother could love," Walker says, and we laugh. But we are both in awe. It is the beginning of something, any idiot can see that. But what may be harder to see is that it is also a great and epic continuation.

While we watch, the almost-pelican cracks through the eggshell, furious for life. Then it shakes off the bits of shell and steps out into a new and unknown world.

(2006)

SY MONTGOMERY

DEEP INTELLECT

Inside the mind of the octopus

ON AN UNSEASONABLY warm day in the middle of March, I traveled from New Hampshire to the moist, dim sanctuary of the New England Aquarium, hoping to touch an alternate reality. I came to meet Athena, the aquarium's forty-pound, five-foot-long, two-and-a-half-year-old giant Pacific octopus.

For me, it was a momentous occasion. I have always loved octopuses. No sci-fi alien is so startlingly strange. Here is someone who, even if she grows to one hundred pounds and stretches more than eight feet long, could still squeeze her boneless body through an opening the size of an orange; an animal whose eight arms are covered with thousands of suckers that taste as well as feel; a mollusk with a beak like a parrot and venom like a snake and a tongue covered with teeth; a creature who can shape-shift, change color, and squirt ink. But most intriguing of all, recent research indicates that octopuses are remarkably intelligent.

Many times I have stood mesmerized by an aquarium tank, wondering, as I stared into the horizontal pupils of an octopus's large, prominent eyes, if she was staring back at me—and if so, what was she thinking?

Not long ago, a question like this would have seemed foolish, if not crazy. How can an octopus *know* anything, much less form an opinion? Octopuses are, after all, "only" invertebrates—they don't even belong with the insects, some of whom, like dragonflies and dung beetles, at least seem to show some smarts. Octopuses are classified within the invertebrates in the mollusk family, and many mollusks, like clams, have no brain.

Only recently have scientists accorded chimpanzees, so closely related to humans we can share blood transfusions, the dignity of having a mind. But now, increasingly, researchers who study octopuses are convinced that these boneless, alien animals—creatures whose ancestors diverged from the lineage that would lead to ours roughly 500 to 700 million years ago—have developed intelligence, emotions, and individual personalities. Their findings are challenging our understanding of consciousness itself.

I had always longed to meet an octopus. Now was my chance: senior aquarist Scott Dowd arranged an introduction. In a back room, he would open the top of Athena's tank. If she consented, I could touch her. The heavy lid covering her tank separated our two worlds. One world was mine and yours, the reality of air and land, where we lumber through life governed by a backbone and constrained by jointed limbs and gravity. The other world was hers, the reality of a nearly gelatinous being breathing water and moving weightlessly through it. We think of our world as the "real" one, but Athena's is realer still: after all, most of the world is ocean, and most animals live there. Regardless of whether they live on land or water, more than 95 percent of all animals are invertebrates, like Athena.

The moment the lid was off, we reached for each other. She had already oozed from the far corner of her lair, where she had been hiding, to the top of the tank to investigate her visitor. Her eight arms boiled up, twisting, slippery, to meet mine. I plunged both my arms elbow deep into the fifty-seven-degree water. Athena's melon-sized head bobbed to the surface. Her left eye (octopuses have one dominant eye like humans have a dominant hand) swiveled in its socket to meet mine. "She's looking at you," Dowd said.

As we gazed into each other's eyes, Athena encircled my arms with hers, latching on with first dozens, then hundreds of her sensitive, dexterous suckers. Each arm has more than two hundred of them. The famous naturalist and explorer William Beebe found the touch of the octopus repulsive. "I have always a struggle before I can make my hands do their duty and seize a tentacle," he confessed. But to me, Athena's suckers felt like an alien's kiss—at once a probe and a caress. Although an octopus can taste with all of its skin, in the suckers both taste and touch are exquisitely developed. Athena was tasting me and feeling me at once, knowing my skin, and possibly the blood and bone beneath, in a way I could never fathom.

When I stroked her soft head with my fingertips, she changed color beneath my touch, her ruby-flecked skin going white and smooth. This, I learned, is a sign of a relaxed octopus. An agitated giant Pacific octopus turns red, its skin gets pimply, and it erects two papillae over the eyes, which some divers say look like horns. One name for the species is "devil fish." With sharp, parrotlike beaks, octopuses can bite, and most have neurotoxic, flesh-dissolving venom. The pressure from an octopus's suckers can tear flesh (one scientist calculated that to break the hold of the suckers of the much smaller common octopus would require a quarter ton of force). One volunteer who interacted with an octopus left the aquarium with arms covered in red hickeys.

Occasionally an octopus takes a dislike to someone.

One of Athena's predecessors at the aquarium, Truman, felt this way about a female volunteer. Using his funnel, the siphon near the side of the head used to jet through the sea, Truman would shoot a soaking stream of salt water at this young woman whenever he got a chance. Later, she quit her volunteer position for college. But when she returned to visit several months later, Truman, who hadn't squirted anyone in the meanwhile, took one look at her and instantly soaked her again.

Athena was remarkably gentle with me—even as she began to transfer her grip from her smaller, outer suckers to the larger ones. She seemed to be slowly but steadily pulling me into her tank. Had it been big enough to accommodate my body, I would have gone in willingly. But at this point, I asked Dowd if perhaps I should try to detach from some of the suckers. With his help, Athena and I pulled gently apart.

I was honored that she appeared comfortable with me. But what did she know about me that informed her opinion? When Athena looked into my eyes, what was she thinking?

While Alexa Warburton was researching her senior thesis at Middlebury College's newly created octopus lab, "every day," she said, "was a disaster."

She was working with two species: the California two-spot, with a head the size of a clementine, and the smaller, Florida species, *Octopus joubini*. Her objective was to study the octopuses' behavior in a T-shaped maze. But her study subjects were constantly thwarting her.

The first problem was keeping the octopuses alive. The four-hundred-gallon tank was divided into separate compartments for each animal. But even though students hammered in dividers, the octopuses found ways to dig beneath them—and eat each other. Or they'd mate, which is equally lethal.

Octopuses die after mating and laying eggs, but first they go senile, acting like a person with dementia. "They swim loop-the-loop in the tank, they look all googly-eyed, they won't look you in the eye or attack prey," Warburton said. One senile octopus crawled out of the tank, squeezed into a crack in the wall, dried up, and died.

It seemed to Warburton that some of the octopuses were purposely uncooperative. To run the T-maze, the pre-veterinary student had to scoop an animal from its tank with a net and transfer it to a bucket. With bucket firmly covered, octopus and researcher would take the elevator down to the room with the maze. Some octopuses did not like being removed from their tanks. They would hide. They would squeeze into a corner where they couldn't be pried out. They would hold on to some object with their arms and not let go.

Some would let themselves be captured, only to use the net as a trampoline. They'd leap off the mesh and onto the floor—and then run for it. Yes, *run*. "You'd chase them under the tank, back and forth, like you were chasing a cat," Warburton said. "It's so *weird!*"

Octopuses in captivity actually escape their watery enclosures with alarming frequency. While on the move, they have been discovered on carpets, along bookshelves, in a teapot, and inside the aquarium tanks of other fish—upon whom they have usually been dining.

Even though the Middlebury octopuses were disaster prone, Warburton liked certain individuals very much. Some, she said, "would lift their arms out of the water like dogs jump up to greet you." Though in their research papers the students refer to each octopus by a number, the students named them all. One of the *joubini* was such a problem they named her The Bitch. "Catching her for the maze always took twenty minutes," Warburton said. "She'd grip onto something and not let go. Once she got stuck in a filter and we couldn't get her out. It was awful!"

Then there was Wendy. Warburton used Wendy as part of her thesis presentation, a formal event that was videotaped. First Wendy squirted salt water at her, drenching her nice suit. Then, as Warburton tried to show how octopuses use the T-maze, Wendy scurried to the bottom of the tank and hid in the sand. Warburton says the whole debacle occurred because the octopus realized in advance what was going to happen. "Wendy," she said, "just didn't feel like being caught in the net."

Data from Warburton's experiments showed that the California two-spots quickly learned which side of a T-maze offered a terra-cotta pot to hide in. But Warburton learned far more than her experiments revealed. "Science," she says, "can only say so much. I know they watched me. I know they sometimes followed me. But they are so different from anything we normally study. How do you prove the intelligence of someone so different?"

Measuring the minds of other creatures is a perplexing problem. One yardstick scientists use is brain size, since humans have big brains. But size doesn't always match smarts. As is well known in electronics, anything can be miniaturized. Small brain size was the evidence once used to argue that birds were stupid—before some birds were proven intelligent enough to compose music, invent dance steps, ask questions, and do math.

Octopuses have the largest brains of any invertebrate. Athena's is the size of a walnut—as big as the brain of the famous African gray parrot, Alex, who learned to use more than one hundred spoken words meaningfully. That's proportionally bigger than the brains of most of the largest dinosaurs.

Another measure of intelligence: you can count neurons.

The common octopus has about 130 million of them in its brain. A human has 100 billion. But this is where things get weird. Three-fifths of an octopus's neurons are not in the brain; they're in its arms.

"It is as if each arm has a mind of its own," says Peter Godfrey-Smith, a diver, professor of philosophy at the Graduate Center of the City University of New York, and an admirer of octopuses. For example, researchers who cut off an octopus's arm (which the octopus can regrow) discovered that not only does the arm crawl away on its own, but if the arm meets a food item, it seizes it—and tries to pass it to where the mouth would be if the arm were still connected to its body.

"Meeting an octopus," writes Godfrey-Smith, "is like meeting an intelligent alien." Their intelligence sometimes even involves changing colors and shapes. One video online shows a mimic octopus alternately morphing into a flatfish, several sea snakes, and a lionfish by changing color, altering the texture of its skin, and shifting the position of its body. Another video shows an octopus materializing from a clump of algae. Its skin exactly matches the alg ae from which it seems to bloom—until it swims away.

For its color palette, the octopus uses three layers of three different types of cells near the skin's surface. The deepest layer passively reflects background light. The topmost may contain the colors yellow, red, brown, and black. The middle layer shows an array of glittering blues, greens, and golds. But how does an octopus decide what animal to mimic, what colors to turn? Scientists have no idea, especially given that octopuses are likely *colorblind*.

But new evidence suggests a breathtaking possibility. Woods Hole Marine Biological Laboratory and University of Washington researchers found that the skin of the cuttlefish *Sepia officinalis*, a color-changing cousin of octopuses, contains gene sequences usually expressed only in the light-sensing retina of the eye. In other words, cephalopods—octopuses, cuttlefish, and squid—may be able to see with their skin.

The American philosopher Thomas Nagel once wrote a famous paper titled "What Is It Like to Be a Bat?" Bats can see with sound. Like dolphins, they can locate their prey using echoes. Nagel concluded it was impossible to know what it's like to be a bat. And a bat is a fellow mammal like us—not someone who tastes with its suckers, sees with its skin, and whose severed arms can wander about, each with a mind of its own. Nevertheless, there are researchers still working diligently to understand what it's like to be an octopus.

Jennifer Mather spent most of her time in Bermuda floating facedown on the surface of the water at the edge of the sea. Breathing through a snorkel, she was watching *Octopus vulgaris*—the common octopus. Although indeed common (they are found in tropical and temperate waters worldwide), at the time of her study in the mid-1980s, "nobody knew what they were doing."

In a relay with other students from six-thirty in the morning till six-thirty at night, Mather worked to find out. Sometimes she'd see an octopus hunting. A hunting expedition could take five minutes or three hours. The octopus would capture something, inject it with venom, and carry it home to eat. "Home," Mather found, is where octopuses spend most of their time. A home, or den, which an octopus may occupy only a few days before switching to a new one, is a place where the shell-less octopus can safely hide: a hole in a rock, a discarded shell, or a cubbyhole in a sunken ship. One species, the Pacific red octopus, particularly likes to den in stubby, brown, glass beer bottles.

One octopus Mather was watching had just returned

home and was cleaning the front of the den with its arms. Then, suddenly, it left the den, crawled a meter away, picked up one particular rock and placed the rock in front of the den. Two minutes later, the octopus ventured forth to select a second rock. Then it chose a third. Attaching suckers to all the rocks, the octopus carried the load home, slid through the den opening, and carefully arranged the three objects in front. Then it went to sleep. What the octopus was thinking seemed obvious: "Three rocks are enough. Good night!"

The scene has stayed with Mather. The octopus "must have had some concept," she said, "of what it wanted to make itself feel safe enough to go to sleep." And the octopus knew how to get what it wanted: by employing foresight, planning—and perhaps even tool use. Mather is the lead author of *Octopus: The Ocean's Intelligent Invertebrate*, which includes observations of octopuses who dismantle Lego sets and open screw-top jars. Coauthor Roland Anderson reports that octopuses even learned to open the childproof caps on Extra Strength Tylenol pill bottles—a feat that eludes many humans with university degrees.

In another experiment, Anderson gave octopuses plastic pill bottles painted different shades and with different textures to see which evoked more interest. Usually each octopus would grasp a bottle to see if it were edible and then cast it off. But to his astonishment, Anderson saw one of the octopuses doing something striking: she was blowing carefully modulated jets of water from her funnel to send the bottle to the other end of her aquarium, where the water flow sent it back to her. She repeated the action twenty times. By the eighteenth time, Anderson was already on the phone with Mather with the news: "She's bouncing the ball!"

This octopus wasn't the only one to use the bottle as a toy. Another octopus in the study also shot water at the bottle, sending it back and forth across the water's surface, rather than circling the tank. Anderson's observations were reported in the *Journal of Comparative Psychology.* "This fit all the criteria for play behavior," said Anderson. "Only intelligent animals play—animals like crows and chimps, dogs and humans."

Aquarists who care for octopuses feel that not only *can* these animals play with toys, but they may *need* to play with toys. An *Octopus Enrichment Handbook* has been developed by Cincinnati's Newport Aquarium, with ideas of how to keep these creatures entertained. One suggestion is to hide food inside Mr. Potato Head and let your octopus dismantle it. At the Seattle Aquarium, giant Pacific octopuses play with a baseball-sized plastic ball that can be screwed together by twisting the two halves. Sometimes the mollusks screw the halves back together after eating the prey inside.

At the New England Aquarium, it took an engineer who worked on the design of cubic zirconium to devise a puzzle worthy of a brain like Athena's. Wilson Menashi, who began volunteering at the aquarium weekly after retiring from the Arthur D. Little Corporation sixteen years ago, devised a series of three Plexiglas cubes, each with a different latch. The smallest cube has a sliding latch that twists to lock down, like the bolt on a horse stall. Aquarist Bill Murphy puts a crab inside the clear cube and leaves the lid open. Later he lets the octopus lift open the lid. Finally he locks the lid, and invariably the octopus figures out how to open it.

Next he locks the first cube within a second one. The new latch slides counterclockwise to catch on a bracket. The third box is the largest, with two different locks: a bolt that slides into position to lock down, and a second one like a lever arm, sealing the lid much like the top of an old-fashioned glass canning jar.

All the octopuses Murphy has known learned fast. They typically master a box within two or three once-a-week tries.

"Once they 'get it,'" he says, "they can open it very fast"—within three or four minutes. But each may use a different strategy.

George, a calm octopus, opened the boxes methodically. The impetuous Gwenevere squeezed the second-largest box so hard she broke it, leaving a hole two inches wide. Truman, Murphy said, was "an opportunist." One day, inside the smaller of the two boxes, Murphy put two crabs, who started to fight. Truman was too excited to bother with locks. He poured his seven-foot-long body through the two-inch crack Gwenevere had made, and visitors looked into his exhibit to find the giant octopus squeezed, suckers flattened, into the tiny space between the walls of the fourteen-cubic-inch box outside and the six-cubic-inch one inside it. Truman stayed inside half an hour. He never opened the inner box—probably he was too cramped.

Three weeks after I had first met Athena, I returned to the aquarium to meet the man who had designed the cubes. Menashi, a quiet grandfather with a dark moustache, volunteers every Tuesday. "He has a real way with octopuses," Dowd and Murphy told me. I was eager to see how Athena behaved with him.

Murphy opened the lid of her tank, and Athena rose to the surface eagerly. A bucket with a handful of fish sat nearby. Did she rise so eagerly sensing the food? Or was it the sight of her friend that attracted her? "She knows me," Menashi answered softly.

Anderson's experiments with giant Pacific octopuses in Seattle prove Menashi is right. The study exposed eight octopuses to two unfamiliar humans, dressed identically in blue aquarium shirts. One person consistently fed a particular octopus, and another always touched it with a bristly stick. Within a week, at first sight of the people, most octopuses moved toward the feeders and away from the irritators, at whom they occasionally aimed their water-shooting funnels.

Upon seeing Menashi, Athena reached up gently and grasped his hands and arms. She flipped upside down, and he placed a capelin in some of the suckers near her mouth, at the center of her arms. The fish vanished. After she had eaten, Athena floated in the tank upside down, like a puppy asking for a belly rub. Her arms twisted lazily. I took one in my hand to feel the suckers—did that arm know it had hold of a different person than the other arms did? Her grip felt calm, relaxed. With me, earlier, she seemed playful, exploratory, excited. The way she held Menashi with her suckers seemed to me like the way a long-married couple holds hands at the movies.

I leaned over the tank to look again into her eyes, and she bobbed up to return my gaze. "She has eyelids like a person does," Menashi said. He gently slid his hand near one of her eyes, causing her to slowly wink.

Biologists have long noted the similarities between the eyes of an octopus and the eyes of a human. Canadian zoologist N. J. Berrill called it "the single most startling feature of the whole animal kingdom" that these organs are nearly identical: both animals' eyes have transparent corneas, regulate light with iris diaphragms, and focus lenses with a ring of muscle.

Scientists are currently debating whether we and octopuses evolved eyes separately, or whether a common ancestor had the makings of the eye. But intelligence is another matter. "The same thing that got them their smarts isn't the same thing that got us our smarts," says Mather, "because our two ancestors didn't *have* any smarts." Half a billion years ago, the brainiest thing on the planet had only a few neurons. Octopus and human intelligence evolved independently.

"Octopuses," writes philosopher Godfrey-Smith, "are a

separate experiment in the evolution of the mind." And that, he feels, is what makes the study of the octopus mind so philosophically interesting.

The octopus mind and the human mind probably evolved for different reasons. Humans—like other vertebrates whose intelligence we recognize (parrots, elephants, and whales)— are long-lived, social beings. Most scientists agree that an important event that drove the flowering of our intelligence was when our ancestors began to live in social groups. Decoding and developing the many subtle relationships among our fellows, and keeping track of these changing relationships over the course of the many decades of a typical human lifespan, was surely a major force shaping our minds.

But octopuses are neither long-lived nor social. Athena, to my sorrow, may live only a few more months—the natural lifespan of a giant Pacific octopus is only three years. If the aquarium added another octopus to her tank, one might eat the other. Except to mate, most octopuses have little to do with others of their kind.

So why is the octopus so intelligent? What is its mind *for*? Mather thinks she has the answer. She believes the event driving the octopus toward intelligence was the loss of the ancestral shell. Losing the shell freed the octopus for mobility. Now they didn't need to wait for food to find them; they could hunt like tigers. And while most octopuses love crab best, they hunt and eat dozens of other species—each of which demands a different hunting strategy. Each animal you hunt may demand a different skill set: Will you camouflage yourself for a stalk-and-ambush attack? Shoot through the sea for a fast chase? Or crawl out of the water to capture escaping prey?

Losing the protective shell was a trade-off. Just about anything big enough to eat an octopus will do so. Each species of predator also demands a different evasion strategy—from flashing warning coloration if your attacker is vulnerable to venom, to changing color and shape to camouflage, to fortifying the door to your home with rocks.

Such intelligence is not always evident in the laboratory. "In the lab, you give the animals this situation, and they react," points out Mather. But in the wild, "the octopus is actively discovering his environment, not waiting for it to hit him. The animal makes the decision to go out and get information, figures out how to get the information, gathers it, uses it, stores it. This has a great deal to do with consciousness."

So what does it feel like to be an octopus? Philosopher Godfrey-Smith has given this a great deal of thought, especially when he meets octopuses and their relatives, giant cuttlefish, on dives in his native Australia. "They come forward and look at you. They reach out to touch you with their arms," he said. "It's remarkable how little is known about them . . . but I could see it turning out that we have to change the way we think of the nature of the mind itself to take into account minds with less of a centralized self."

"I think consciousness comes in different flavors," agrees Mather. "Some may have consciousness in a way we may not be able to imagine."

In May, I visited Athena a third time. I wanted to see if she recognized me. But how could I tell? Scott Dowd opened the top of her tank for me. Athena had been in a back corner but floated immediately to the top, arms outstretched, upside down.

This time I offered her only one arm. I had injured a knee and, feeling wobbly, used my right hand to steady me while I stood on the stool to lean over the tank. Athena in turn gripped me with only one of her arms, and very few of her suckers. Her hold on me was remarkably gentle.

I was struck by this, since Murphy and others had first

described Athena's personality to me as "feisty." "They earn their names," Murphy had told me. Athena is named for the Greek goddess of wisdom, war, and strategy. She is not usually a laid-back octopus, like George had been. "Athena could pull you into the tank," Murphy had warned. "She's curious about what you are."

Was she less curious now? Did she remember me? I was disappointed that she did not bob her head up to look at me. But perhaps she didn't need to. She may have known from the taste of my skin who I was. But why was this feisty octopus hanging in front of me in the water, upside down?

Then I thought I might know what she wanted from me. She was begging. Dowd asked around and learned that Athena hadn't eaten in a couple of days, then allowed me the thrilling privilege of handing her a capelin.

Perhaps I had understood something basic about what it felt like to be Athena at that moment: she was hungry. I handed a fish to one of her larger suckers, and she began to move it toward her mouth. But soon she brought more arms to the task, and covered the fish with many suckers—as if she were licking her fingers, savoring the meal.

A week after I last visited Athena, I was shocked to receive this e-mail from Scott Dowd: "Sorry to write with some sad news. Athena appears to be in her final days, or even hours. She will live on, though, through your conveyance." Later that same day, Dowd wrote to tell me that she had died. To my surprise, I found myself in tears.

Why such sorrow? I had understood from the start that octopuses don't live very long. I also knew that while Athena did seem to recognize me, I was not by any means her special friend. But she was very significant to me, both as an individual and as a representative from her octopodan world. She had given me a great gift: a deeper understanding of what it means to think, to feel, and to know. I was eager to meet more of her kind.

And so, it was with some excitement that I read this e-mail from Dowd a few weeks later: "There is a young pup octopus headed to Boston from the Pacific Northwest. Come shake hands (x8) when you can."

(2011)

J.B. MACKINNON

WISDOM IN THE WILD

A case for elderly animals

THE ONLY ASPECT of my life that I can trace directly to my maternal grandmother is my recent decision to stop eating groundfish. I have never been particularly close to her, mostly due to geography, and in place of any real relationship what has remained remarkable to me is her age. She is 104 years old.

My elders in general are like figments of the information age: I have knowledge of them, but little experience. This hardly makes me exceptional among recent generations, and yet the consequences of growing up without elders are re-markably unclear in a society where their contributions are often seen as optional.

My grandmother's short-term memory has failed her, and it is too late to ask how she feels about groundfish; the synap-tic link between the two is mine alone. I made the connection in a lecture hall as I listened to a marine biologist describe the planet's most remote fisheries, which target species such as orange roughy and Patagonian toothfish (marketed as "Chil-ean sea bass") on the slopes of underwater mountains. "Irreplaceable fuel is being burned to catch irreplaceable fish to bring to market at a net loss," he said.

The fuel is irreplaceable, of course, only in the sense that fossil fuels are not replenished in the earth's crust within meaningful human timelines. The fish he's referring to, which live near the ocean floor and increasingly end up in the frozen foods aisle, are irreplaceable for much the same reason—the average seamount groundfish is estimated to be one hundred years old.

I have stopped eating groundfish, not because the fishery is unsustainable, which was the biologist's actual point, but because any one of the fish might be as old as my grand-mother. The decision is easy to deride as a most-embarrassing anthropomorphism, I know, but my spouse, at least, offered unhesitating support. "Who knows what wisdom they've developed in that time?" she said. And who wants to risk con-suming the planet's store of wisdom?

There may be more to that way of thinking than prima facie absurdism and overweening sensitivity. In 1993, a severe drought struck Tarangire National Park in Tanzania. In a typi-cal wet season, more than two feet of water would have swept the savannah, greening the sepia landscape, but that year less than three inches would fall. The drought was a crisis for the park's African elephants, with their elephantine appetites for vegetation and water. By the time the rains came again, the Tarangire herd had lost sixteen out of eighty-one calves, a level of juvenile mortality ten times above normal.

The deaths were not evenly distributed. The Tarangire el-ephants belonged to twenty-one different family groups under the umbrellas of three clans, identified for research purposes as clans A, B, and C. Fully 70 percent of the total calf deaths were sustained by clan B. The fatal distinction seemed to be that clan B had remained within the park boundaries, while clans A and C left the park to seek water farther afield.

Charles Foley, an elephant biologist working in Tarangire, asked the obvious question: Why did clan B fail to leave the park? He found the only convincing answer in the ages of the females—known in the field as matriarchs—that lead the family groups. Elephants can live to be more than sixty years old in the wild, but clan B's oldest matriarch was barely middle aged, in her early thirties. Only clans A and C had females old enough that they may have remembered the area's previous drought, which had lasted two years beginning in 1958. "It might thus be possible," wrote Foley in the cautious language of new discovery, "that clan B remained within the park during the 1993 drought because the sole surviving older female lacked knowledge of areas with forage and water outside the park, while older matriarchs in the other clans were able to lead their groups, and probably other groups within the clan, to such refugia using their previous experience to guide them." Unstated but implied in Foley's research is the fact that the elephants' ability to survive depends on an unbroken thread of learning reaching deeply back in time. Severe drought tends to strike Tarangire only every fifty years or so. To maintain a mental map of those lifesaving water holes over centuries demands the continuous presence not merely of adult elephants, but of elderly ones.

There is a more familiar way to think about older animals, and it is captured in a quotation from that early twentieth-century chronicler of legendary beasts, Ernest Thompson Seton: "No wild animal dies of old age." Ask yourself what predators eat, and there is a textbook answer at hand: they eat the young, the sick, and the old. A role for aged animals, then, but surely not a fortunate one.

Seton himself saw more nuance than that. Among his less frequently cited observations is that, once an animal has survived perilous youth, "he is likely to outlive his prime." *Wild Animals I Have Known,* the book that made Seton famous, is first and foremost a collection of stories about aged animals. There stands Old Lobo, the leader of a wolf pack in the Corrumpa Valley of New Mexico—a place where no wolves at all live today—and an animal of such world-wise experience and force of personality that he gathers Seton's poisoned baits (so carefully prepared to prevent any telltale human scent that the author had cut the meat with a bone knife while wearing gloves "steeped in the hot blood of the heifer"), piles them up, and, if I am reading the euphemisms correctly, shits on them. Another of Seton's characters is Silverspot the crow, not with a "delicate blue iris," but the "dark brown eye of the old stager." Seton recalls a saying of his times: "Wise as an old crow."

How old can a crow be, anyway? Does it come as some surprise that they frequently manage thirty or forty years, and that the age of eighty is not unheard of? Albatrosses and parrots have also been known to live into their eighties, certain salamanders may live more than a century, and queen ants can manage nearly thirty years. House sparrows, ubiquitous in cities and towns across North America and Europe, may weather more than twenty years of life, and gray squirrels can outlive many dogs. For the most part, though, these numbers are conjectural, based on limited samples or zookeepers' records. Bob Paine, who for more than forty years has studied the ecology of Tatoosh Island off the Olympic Peninsula in Washington State, has observed one *Urticina crassicornis,* a common shoreline anemone, since his first trip to the island in 1968. "It was old then, probably," he tells me, "and is older now."

If we know little about the ages of things, then the record is even more scant when it comes to the ornate variety of aging in the wild. We might see a familiar portrait in an old baboon, his fur dull and teeth worn as he appraises the pass-

ing young females with watery eyes, his most audible contribution to the daily dramas of the troop little more than the
occasional fart. In other cases, though, the advance of years is
enviably invisible to human eyes. Many birds remain just as
iridescent, just as marvelously preened, at the farthest reaches
of senescence as when they were newly fledged. Old spinner
dolphins appear perfectly capable of performing that species'
eponymous acrobatics. One day they simply die.

Perhaps most poignantly, it is often in older age that
humans and animals reach out to one another across species.
One can suggest motivations ranging from loneliness and
boredom to the self-interest of animals that see nothing left to
lose, and some security to gain, in living alongside a species
that their predators avoid. Whatever the reasons, the bond
can go far beyond the stereotype of old folks tossing bread
crumbs to pigeons in the park. Near a pond in Blockley, England, stands a tombstone that reads, "In Memory of the Old
Fish." It was set there in the name of William Keyte, a retired
wheelwright who developed a relationship with one particular
trout, which would rise whenever its fellow elder approached
the shore. At times the fish would eat from Keyte's hand; at
others, presumably, the pair would simply pass some time
regarding one another across the infinite divide between
species. The trout died on April 20, 1855, aged an estimated
twenty years. According to a British writer who visited the site
in modern times, "It is said that it was murdered."

The much more enduring tradition is simple indiffer-
ence. If we reject and dread our own advance of years and
buy Harley-Davidson motorcycles in rebellion, when it comes
to old age in the natural world we manage a striking lack of
awareness. In 2009, Anne Innis Dagg published *The Social
Behavior of Older Animals*, one of the rare academic titles
dedicated to aged beasts. In it she admits that her own early

fieldwork with camels and giraffes reported almost nothing about the elders of the species, an omission that she found to be widespread in scientific papers.

Ignorance tends to have consequences, and here we might revisit the pachyderms, this time in apartheid-era South Africa. In the early 1980s, the elephant population was swelling in Kruger National Park, and wildlife managers decided to dart numbers of adult elephants from the air and then shoot them to death on the ground, often in plain view of the juveniles. The youngsters were then rounded up and sent to other parks and reserves, with about forty ending up in Pilanesberg National Park, several hundred miles to the southwest. It must have seemed like a logical if gruesome act of conservation: reduce overpopulation in one place and spread the wealth of the species to others.

More than a decade later, field biologists in Pilanesberg noted what they termed a "novel situation" emerging. White rhinoceros, a species that had been bred back from the brink of extinction, appeared to be suffering, for the first time on record, high mortality from elephant attacks. Between 1992 and 1998, elephants were suspected in the deaths of forty-nine rhinos—a massacre.

The culprits turned out to be the orphaned young males from Kruger. The empathetic conclusion to leap to would be that the elephants' berserk behavior was rooted in the trauma they'd endured as calves, and in fact there is no way to rule out that possibility. As in Tarangire, however, the investigation turned in time to a question of generations.

As they approach maturity, male elephants enter a rutting condition known as *musth*, during which testosterone floods their systems so fiercely that even their posture is changed. The adolescent males in Pilanesberg were entering musth too young and staying in it too long; one suspected rhino killer was finally culled after remaining in musth for as many as five months, a length of time that would be unusual even for a male twice its age. Under more natural circumstances—that is, in an elephant herd not composed of transplanted and possibly traumatized orphans—the adolescent musth periods are cut short by apparently withering encounters with larger, older males. After standing down to a dominant male, the rush of hormones stops, in some cases in a matter of minutes.

As a test, six older male elephants were introduced to Pilanesberg. The killing of rhinoceroses ceased, and the outbreak of elephantine violence was blamed on "a lack of adult supervision," but more particularly, a lack of elders. Elephants are one of the few species in which the importance of older animals is coming to be acknowledged. Without them, the Pilanesberg orphans acted in a way so far outside of pachyderm norms that it seems fair to label it insane.

Evidence of the preferential hunting of the oldest animals—easy to find, meaty, often less dangerous than in their prime—reaches back at least to the Middle Stone Age, and today harvesting by humans is the leading cause of adult mortality in an increasing number of species. In the case of the African elephants, the "behemoths"—matriarchs and patriarchs in the sixth and seventh decades—have already been decimated, and the remaining elders remain the choice of poachers seeking larger ivory tusks.

But in many ways, our greatest experiment in mining the rock of ages is currently underway in the sea. We think of the oceans as mysterious, and they are: so fluid in their connectivity that they make a ready-made metaphor for consciousness. We think of them as ancient, and the oceans are that, too. Long life is a survival strategy in the comfortless deeps, where the continuation of the species often hinges on a simple capacity to endure. In many cases, though, the wondrous breadth of the life aquatic seems as arbitrary as our own. Bowhead whales still wash ashore with two-hundred-year-old harpoon points wedged in their bones, while in 2007 researchers from Bangor University in Wales dredged up a quahog clam estimated by its shell rings to be just over four centuries old, and doomed to be dissected—oh irony!—for what it might teach us about how to slow human aging. Do these maritime elders gather sagacity, each within the limited operating system that it has? Do they perfect existence over their staggering life spans? No one knows. We don't know the wisdom of a centenarian groundfish any more than we do the consequences of bringing an end to the age of old age, in our own societies or the wider world.

Occasionally, there are glimpses. In the first years of the 1990s, the fisheries scientist George Rose headed for the Grand Banks of Newfoundland to attempt to record, for the first time, the migration routes of cod in the northwest Atlantic. The knowledge was suddenly urgent—the fishery, long a symbol of the baroque abundance of which nature is capable, appeared to be failing. Rose predicted the likely migratory path based on water temperatures and sea bottom topography, and echo sounders proved his forecast was largely correct. The fish were there. But he also made an observation he had not expected.

Cod are groundfish, and though they don't live long enough to be contemporaries of my grandmother, they still can reach about twenty-five years of age. It was these big, old fish that seized Rose's attention. He could see them on the echo sounder readouts, individual black smudges at the head of every school. Scouts, his team called them. In most of the schools, there were only a few left.

Rose came ashore with many questions. What signposts did the old cod follow through the vast, undifferentiated space of the sea? How did they determine where and when the schools would spawn? Was he really watching fish that had the wisdom and memory of years, that were keepers of knowledge passed down through generations?

Answers would not be forthcoming. In 1993, the cod stocks collapsed. You could still find cod on the Grand Banks, says Rose, but they were little things, never more than five years old. And for the first time in five hundred years of written history, the ancient migration failed to take place.

(2011)

KATHLEEN JAMIE

STORM PETREL

A flight of imagination on the back of a bird

WE FOUND IT on Rona the very day we'd arrived, and, in keeping it, maybe I imagined I could bring home something of the sky and spaciousness of that island, at least for a while.

It wasn't the dead bird we saw, lying on the turf, not at first, but a tiny wink of metal. I said, "Look, what's that?" and Stuart replied, "Storm petrel. They breed here. But ringed—that's a real find."

So here it is on my desk, in a polyethylene sample bag. An ex–storm petrel, just a clump of desiccated feather and bone, with a tiny ring on its hooked-up leg. When you report a ringed bird it's called a "recovery," but this one was beyond all hope of that.

My five-volume wartime *Handbook of British Birds* says that storm petrels are "essentially pelagic," they "never occur inland except as storm-driven waifs." That's the kind of language they inspire. There's a lovely poem by Richard Murphy, called "Storm Petrel," that begins:

> *Gypsy of the sea,*
> *in winter wambling over scurvy whaleroads*
> *jooking in the wake of ships . . .*

At only six inches long, dark brown with a white rump, somewhat like a house martin, you'd think them too small to jook anywhere at all, never mind in storms, but they manage fine, and come ashore only to breed, in crannies between stones, on islands and cliffs at the ocean's edge.

So the bird is small and the ring on its leg even smaller. Back at the shelter we had to peer at it down the wrong end of binoculars to make out the number and that terse, famous address: "British Museum London S7."

The rings on other birds, bigger birds, gulls and suchlike, often have space for the word *inform*. "Inform British Museum," they say, which makes it sound as though the bird in question had transgressed somehow, had jumped parole. The *inform* makes the bird-ringing project sound imperious and Edwardian, which it was—Edwardian, anyway, because bird ringing began in 1909. But the storm petrel's leg is so twig thin, there is no room for an *inform*.

A few days after we got home, I did contact the British Museum through its website. There is a form with boxes to fill in:

Ring number: 2333551
Type of bird (if known): Storm petrel.
Sex of bird (if known): Unknown.
Age of bird (if known): Unknown.
Was the bird dead or alive? Dead. *Recently (one week)?*
    Long dead. Desiccated corpse.
What had happened to the bird (hit by a car, oiled, etc.)?
    Possibly preyed upon.
Where found? Scotland. Island of North Rona.
Where, more precisely? The north-pointing peninsula
    called Fianuis.
When found? Early July.

I pressed "submit," and the form went off on its own mysterious flight, leaving me with the questions not asked:

Smell of bird? Mysterious, musky, like an unguent.

Where found, even more precisely? Under an earthfast rock, on a patch of gravel, almost at the point where the vegetation expires altogether, and the waves pound ashore.

What kind of day? A lively, companionable summer's afternoon, with a sun bright enough to glint on a tiny metal bead and make us notice it, the only man-made object in all that place.

It was the twentieth century before it was ascertained that birds do actually migrate; it seemed so improbable that swallows, for example, flew all the way to southern Africa. They obviously vanished in autumn and reappeared in late spring, but some folks thought they just hid, or hibernated in the bottoms of ponds. Gilbert White frets around the subject of migration; he hedges his bets. When he was writing this letter of 1769, all options were open:

> When I used to rise in a morning last autumn, and see
> the swallows and martins clustering on the chimnies and
> thatch of the neighbouring cottages, I could not help being
> touched with a secret delight, mixed with some degree of
> mortification: with delight, to observe with how much
> ardour and punctuality those poor little birds obeyed the
> strong impulse towards migration, or hiding, imprinted
> on their minds by their great Creator; and with some
> degree of mortification, when I reflected that, after all our
> pains and enquiries, we are yet not quite certain to what
> regions they do migrate; and are still farther embarrassed
> to find some do not actually migrate at all.

Hybernaculum is his word for the winter quarters a swallow repairs to, but where was this hybernaculum? His other words are interesting too. *Embarrassed* and *mortification* almost suggest that the Enlightenment just then dawning, all that science and discovery, might have been driven not by the will to master and possess nature but out of chagrin. As human beings, our ignorance was beginning to shame us, because we didn't know the least things, like where swallows went in winter.

The British Museum passes the forms on to the British Trust for Ornithology (BTO), which organizes bird ringing in the UK. So in due course a computer printout arrived from the BTO. It informed me that the storm petrel had been ringed twenty-four years previously, not on Rona, where we'd found it, but 170 miles northeast of there, on the island of Yell.

Yell—I knew that place. It's one of the northernmost of the Shetland Islands. Only the summer before, I'd been there with my friend Tim; we'd seen killer whales off the cliffs at Noss, and made a road trip north via the chain of ferries, passing farms and small towns and the oil terminal at Sullom Voe. We'd traversed Yell, then taken another ferry to the farther island of Unst and made our way to see the gannetry at Muckle Flugga. That was all one place, stored in one corner in my mind, but Rona was wholly different. Different direction, different culture: uninhabited, remote, and Hebridean. As soon as I read the letter, though, a connection shot between them. Suddenly they were linked by a flight path, straight as an arrow. I knew maps, but not as the storm petrel does.

Perhaps if you were some sort of purist, if you carried a torch for "the wild" and believed in a pristine natural world over and beyond us, you might consider it an intrusion to catch a bird and make it wear a ring or a tag. Perhaps you'd

consider that their man-made burden violates them in a way.
I admit there was something uncomfortable about the metal
ring soldiering on while the bird's corpse withered, but when
I got the chart out, traced the route, measured the distance,
and understood that yes, of course, on a southwest bearing,
you could swoop along certain channels from the North Sea
through to the Atlantic, it was because this one ringed bird
had extended my imagination. The ring showed only that it
was wedded to the sea, and, if anything, the scale of its jour-
neying made it seem even wilder than before.

It was ringing that proved that swallows indeed flew south
and did not stupefy in the bottom of ponds, and ringing too
that showed that storm petrels do the same. They migrate
from Shetland or Rona, or their many other breeding places,
down to the vast pelagic hybernaculum off Namibia and South
Africa. A few come to grief; become small, washed-up bodies
on a faraway shore, some bearing a return address. An address! Ludicrous thing for a storm petrel to carry. "The Ocean"
would be their address, save for those weeks when they're
obliged to creep between stones to breed.

   So that's why I keep the bird's remains here in this room,
my own hybernaculum—if only for a while. It's just a tuft of
feathers in a polyethylene bag, a tiny skull, and that silvery
ring above its shrunken, black, webbed foot. I keep it for the
intimacy, and for the petrel smell: fusty, musky, suggestive of
a distant island in summer. And I keep it out of sheer respect,
because in life, this ounce of a bird made twenty-four return
trips the length of the Atlantic. Twenty-four at least—which is
not bad at all, for a waif, wambling.

(2013)

LISA COUTURIER

DARK HORSE

*For many equines that have served humans
faithfully, an undignified end awaits*

I WENT TO AN AUCTION last Monday. Not an auction for
foreclosed homes. Not an auction for priceless art or jewelry
or land. I went to the New Holland Livestock Auction in the
Amish and Mennonite country of New Holland, Pennsylvania,
where each week horses are sold—though I'd no intention
of buying one. I know a thing or two about horses. I spend a
significant amount of time with them and can groom them,
bathe them, saddle them, walk them, run them on a lead, ride
them, feed them, blanket them, work them in a round pen,
give them medicine, soak their sore hooves, lift and stretch
their hindlegs and forelegs, clean the undersides of their
feet, bandage their legs, and minister to their wounds. But
I could not foresee, in the spare few minutes each horse at
such an auction is given to demonstrate its abilities, personality, strength, or lack thereof (whether young or old, muscled
or thin), that I'd be able to determine whether any particular
horse would be the one for me.

Besides, it was hard to even think at the auction. I took
a seat in the large crowd of people—with the Amish men

wearing straw hats, black pants, and jackets; with the Mennonite men in their black hats and suspendered pants; with
the city slickers from somewhere else and the country folk
from nearby; with children and their grandparents fussing
over spilled sodas. People talked, laughed, visited, ate hotdogs,
Amish pies, and French fries. We all sat sandwiched together
in the steep, gray bleachers that formed an oval around the
dirt ring in which the horses were shown, one after another,
from ten a.m. until midafternoon. A "loose horse" was a horse
that came into the auction ring without a rider; the horses
with riders were called "saddle horses." Loose horses are at a
disadvantage in terms of finding a good home because even
though they are often saddle broke they nonetheless sell for
less without a rider atop them in the ring.

The fate of those horses that entered and exited the ring
quickly—such as one thin copper-colored Thoroughbred mare
I remember—seemed bleak, the implication being that the
horse was barely worth the time it took to auction off. That
particular Thoroughbred mare, whose long, flaxen mane and
tail were braided, must have had someone who had cared
enough for her to make her pretty, perhaps believing this
would help sell her to a good home, where a girl might braid
her once again. Her head hanging low, she slowly walked
around the ring, only once, and then stepped out a side exit. If
there was any bidding for her, I didn't hear or see it.

More than once the black-bearded Mennonite man run-
ning the auction—someone called him Zimmerman—asked
the audience to settle down. Given the noisy crowd and the
loud, stern voice of the auctioneer calling out in rapid-fire suc-
cession the back-and-forth bidding for the animals, I did not
expect the saddle horses to try so hard to do well. Horses are
flight animals; they flee at the unfamiliar; fear is their dominant emotion. But they are social creatures, too. They aim to

please because they've learned to trust, which meant that even
the strong and healthy horses, of which there were many, obe-
diently did as they were told amid the chaos of the auction: *go
forward; go back; turn left, now right; stop, immediately; go fast,
go slow; stand still.* They were willing to do as asked, as they've
been over the centuries—to churn the soil in our fields, to
fight our battles, to run our races until their lungs bleed or
their bones break. This might possibly be their last chance to
perform, and they mustered up that certain nobility and cour-
age possessed by horses, as though they had upon their backs
the Navajo of long ago, the warriors who, before battle, would
whisper into the ears of their horses: *Be brave and nothing will
happen. We will come back safely.*

Before the auction began, I had walked through the barns
adjoining the auction ring where the horses stood tied to
their posts. There are approximately 9 million horses in the
United States, and at the auction there were two hundred of
not necessarily the unwanted but surely the unlucky. Unlucky
because, though I suppose going to a horse auction might
sound like a day in the country—Amish food and horse-drawn
buggies and all that—this particular auction is frequented by
men known as "kill buyers," which, by association, makes
New Holland a kill auction, one of the largest east of the
Mississippi. Kill buyers (KBs) also are called "meat men"—
the men who purchase horses, typically from the major kill
auctions, and deliver them for slaughter, though they also
visit Thoroughbred racetracks and wheel and deal with horse
dealers who've secured horses elsewhere: former show horses
from the hunter/jumper/eventing/dressage worlds whose
unsuspecting owners believe the dealer will place their horses
in good homes; horses listed in newspaper classifieds or on
Craigslist (you can find them for sale for a dollar); surplus les-

son horses; horses that start out at smaller auctions, such as
the Hickory Auction in Pennsylvania, the Camelot Auction in
New Jersey, or any of the other nearly one hundred horse auctions scattered across the U.S. All these places are entry points
for what is termed the "slaughter pipeline"; and those horses
unlucky enough to stay in the pipeline eventually arrive at bigger and potentially more deadly places such as New Holland,
where, the day I attended, the younger Mennonite and Amish
boys managed a parade of breeds and types (drafts, minis,
Quarter Horses, Thoroughbreds, Standardbreds, fit and fat
and healthy horses, tired and skinny horses, carriage horses,
work horses, mares and geldings and stallions and foals) by
whipping in the face the more frightened horses that took
longer than a few seconds to understand what they were being
told to do. Of course, not just KBs attend such auctions. And
the horses being sold could have many possible new homes
and potential uses—with families who want a trail horse, say,
or with horse trainers, or with competitive riders looking for
a strong event or endurance horse. Nonetheless, by the end
of the day at any number of auctions around the country, the
KBs have "bid for horses against private buyers, against each
other and other dealers, as well as against horse rescues,"
says Christy Sheidy of Another Chance 4 Horses, in Bernville,
Pennsylvania. "The horses the kill buyers took could've easily
been re-homed and gone on to live happy lives with families
who want and appreciate them. *They were not unwanted.*"

Ultimately, kill buyers take what they need to satisfy their
contracts with slaughterhouses. The day I visited New Holland,
they were taking horses going for $500 or less; and though
sometimes these were the young or the old, the sick or the
skinny horses, it was clear that the healthy ones were pre-
ferred—the more body weight, the more money for the load.
The buzz at New Holland that day was that a KB would receive

about $600 from the slaughterhouse for each horse, though prices fluctuate depending on location, supply, and demand. A report quoted by a USDA slaughter statistician for that time period indicated the price of a horse at slaughter to be around forty-three cents per pound, but horsemeat can fetch as much as fifteen dollars per pound in the retail market.

Because Americans don't eat horses, it is surprising to learn that people of other cultures do. "Horse meat became popular after World War II," says Carolyn Stull, animal welfare specialist at the School of Veterinary Medicine, University of California, Davis. "It was an inexpensive protein for lower-income people in Europe, where beef was scarce, and old or lame draft horses were processed as affordable meat." Prices have risen since World War II, but the market continues to be highly profitable for the foreign companies that process horses from the U.S. and Canada, both of which have large horse populations. In a paper concerning horse transport regulations, Stull cites the different types of horse meat various cultures prefer. For instance, the Japanese prefer draft horse meat, she writes, referencing a 1999 article titled "Horses Destined to Slaughter" (though at New Holland I heard that the Japanese and French like Quarter Horses the most because of the lean muscle mass). The Italians, cites Stull, prefer eighteen- to twenty-four-month-old horses; the French go for ten- to twelve-year-old horses; and the Swiss take the two- to three-year-olds.

There are currently no horse-slaughtering facilities in the U.S., which means horses are transported to Canada and Mexico before being put to a typically untimely death. In the 1980s there were sixteen slaughterhouses in the U.S. By 1993 there were about ten, scattered across the country—in Connecticut, Texas, Oregon, Illinois, Nebraska, and Ohio. By the fall of 2007, the last three—two in Texas and one in

Illinois—were shut down by courts that upheld state laws ban-
ning horse slaughter. The fight against slaughter within the
U.S. grew from outrage over the fact that ex-racehorses like
Ferdinand, Kentucky Derby winner and Horse of the Year, as
well as a racehorse named Exceller, who'd defeated two Triple
Crown winners, had slipped through the cracks and been
purchased for slaughter overseas (Exceller in Sweden in 1997,
and Ferdinand in Japan in 2002). Slaughter opponents in-
cluded the general public (seven in ten Americans are against
it, according to Madeleine Pickens, former racehorse breeder
and wife of billionaire T. Boone Pickens); a majority of the
Thoroughbred racing industry; and professionals within the
horse industry (trainers, riders, breeders), all of whom, once
they spoke up for horses, were labeled "animal rights activists"
by the pro-slaughter contingency as a way to discredit them.

Slaughter, however, is not banned at the federal level, and
individual states that have not banned it could see new slaughterhouses opened in the future. In early 2009, a Montana
state legislator, aptly named Ed Butcher, tried and failed to
lure the Chinese (who eat a lot of horses) into building a plant
there. But Butcher has not given up. As of March 2010, even
though he decided not to run for re-election, he told a reporter
for the Montana *Independent Record* that he's still "shepherd-
ing his horse slaughterhouse idea by trying to find a market."
According to the *Journal of the American Veterinary Medical
Association*, lawmakers in nearly a dozen states are drafting
initiatives to reintroduce the possibility of slaughtering horses
in the United States. This is why slaughter opponents cease-
lessly fight for the passage of the Prevention of Equine Cruelty
Act of 2009 (H.R. 503 / S. 727), which would end at a national
level the slaughter of horses for human consumption as well
as the domestic and international transport of live horses or
horseflesh for human consumption.

A new plot turn in this story is that, as of July 31, 2010, the European Union (EU) will require that horses destined for slaughter and human consumption are free from certain drugs, including many that long have been in the bodies of horses, most notably phenylbutazone (a pain reliever and anti-inflammatory commonly called "bute," which is given to an estimated 98 percent of American Thoroughbred racehorses as well as to just about any breed of horse to relieve occasional pain or swelling). Kill buyers will be required to provide a signed statement for each horse claiming that to the best of their knowledge the animal has not been treated with these particular substances. "Some kill buyers claim openly that they will simply fill in bogus forms," says John Holland, president of the Equine Welfare Alliance. The fact is, it would be impossible for KBs to tell the truth, because the horses they pick up could have had numerous owners, and it is rare for papers of any kind to travel with horses to auction, let alone an animal's lifelong medical history.

It is unlikely that this new hurdle will suddenly stop kill buyers from shipping horses across our borders, as they had been doing even before the last three U.S. slaughterhouses closed. The figures for 2009 show that horses slaughtered in Canada were sold to as many as twenty-four countries, with France, Switzerland, Japan, and Belgium receiving 92 percent of the exports. The demand from countries where horseflesh is considered a pricey delicacy is the predominant reason horses go to slaughter. Some slaughter proponents suggest that the demand is met by horses that are no longer useful to their owners and are therefore better off slaughtered than suffering starvation and neglect. Neglect does of course occur, but neglected and starving horses are not necessarily the ones chosen by the KBs, and such horses don't always make it to auction to begin with. Consider the nearly two hundred mus-

tangs found starving—seventy-four of them already dead—at
the Three Strikes Ranch in Nebraska in 2009. With such a
large enticement of horseflesh, the owner of Three Strikes
could have chosen to have the meat man come hither; he
could've sent his neglected horses off with a KB who would've
paid him for the animals. But he did not.

It is more often the case that horse owners do not wish
their healthy animals an untimely death, are unaware that
dealers flip their equines like real estate, and would be horri-
fied to know that their animals had been sold into the slaughter pipeline. Bottom line: a horse is a commodity and someone is making money off of it somewhere down the road.
And it is all perfectly legal, since horses are deemed livestock
by the U.S. government, even though they are not part of the
American food chain.

Horses in America today are used less for agricultural
purposes and more for sport, competition, trail rides, and
showing. They are bred and raised to be companions, not din-
ner entrees, which is why slaughter seems incompatible with
our country's relationship to this animal. And the manner in
which these horses are killed only makes it more so. Before
a horse is ostensibly unconscious and hung upside down by
one of its back legs, and before its throat is cut and it is bled
out, the horse must enter the killbox, or knockbox, where it is
shot in the head with a device called a captive bolt gun, which
is a four-inch-long, retractable, nail-like instrument. The captive bolt gun does not immediately kill the horse but is meant
to render it insensible to pain. According to the American
Veterinary Medical Association, a captive bolt gun will work
effectively under the following conditions: if it is clean and in
proper working order, if the horse stands still, and if, shall we
say, the gun is dead-on the right spot on the horse's forehead.
These conditions are hard to ensure.

"It is a dangerous practice to equate the medical procedure of chemical euthanasia performed by a veterinarian to end an animal's life with that of a slaughterhouse worker killing an animal," says Nena Winand, a faculty member in the College of Veterinary Medicine at Cornell University. "There are many differences. Vets monitor vitals to cause the least amount of trauma, mental or otherwise. [Slaughterhouse workers] don't take the time to monitor that the horse is dead. The horse gets hit multiple times with the captive bolt gun. We don't know that they're always insensible to pain. This treatment of horses has been going on since I was a kid, and I'm fifty-two now. The industry has never been successfully regulated. We pay taxes to monitor and enforce the humane treatment of these horses, but nothing's enforced and it never has been. Whoever says otherwise is misrepresenting the history of this industry. To say it's all perfect—well, it's just insane."

It all seems like the ultimate betrayal to a horse that likely served its owners for years and, at some point in its life, experienced human kindness. But there is not an exchange rate for kindness, while there is one for demand. In 2009 alone, demand resulted in the slaughter of 93,812 horses in Canada; of those, 56 percent were American horses; Canada's revenue was $86.9 million; and the largest importer was France, paying $27.8 million. Worth noting, in a reflective and economy-minded sort of way regarding the issue of demand, is something comedian Jon Stewart said, which was referred to by racing columnist Jay Hovdey in the *Daily Racing Form*: "There's demand for cocaine and hookers, too."

"There are two things that flourish in the dark—mushrooms and horse slaughter," said the late John Hettinger, a Thoroughbred racing legend and former member of the board of trustees of the New York Racing Association. "Most people don't know it's going on. We must deny them the darkness."

To shine a light inside the darkness, various humane groups (the Humane Society of the U.S., the Humane Farming Association) have taken undercover videos inside slaughterhouses, where workers poke, whip, and beat the animals' bodies with fiberglass rods. Video from inside Mexican slaughterhouses reveals horses stabbed repeatedly with knives, which paralyzes the horse but leaves it conscious at the start of the slaughter process. The videos are exceedingly difficult to watch. In response to a Freedom of Information Act request, the USDA recently disclosed some nine hundred pages (including photos) documenting hundreds of violations of humane treatment to horses during transport to slaughter and at the American plants prior to their closings in 2007. The photos (available on Kaufmanzoning.net) depict horses with severed legs, crushed skulls, and missing eyes, as well as pregnant mares. Late-term pregnant mares, foals, blind horses, and horses who cannot stand on all four legs are not supposed to be sent to slaughter. Those animals that do make the trip are to be fed, watered, and rested. Often they are not.

"The whole thing, it's a boondoggle on the American people," said slaughter opponent and oilman T. Boone Pickens to a Chicago NBC reporter. "People that are for slaughter should be forced to go down on that kill floor."

For those of us who will never get to the kill floor, or who have not the stomach to watch the videos on YouTube, here are two short excerpts, the first from the notes of an Animal and Plant Health Inspection Investigator at eleven-twenty a.m. on April 13, 2005, at the Cavel slaughter plant in DeKalb, Illinois:

> *Eight horses were in the alleyway leading directly to the knock-box. . . . The employee who is routinely assigned to work on the kill floor, hanging the horses on the rails, was using a riding crop to whip the horse in the alleyway clos-*

*est to the knock-box. This horse continued to move back-
ward, away from the knock-box causing the other horses
behind it to be overcrowded. As the whipping continued
the horses in the alleyway became extremely excited. I
immediately told the employee to stop but he did not listen
to me. During this time, the last horse in the alleyway at-
tempted to jump over the alleyway wall and became stuck
over the top of the wall. Eventually it had flailed around
enough to fall over to the other side of the wall. I went
to the kill floor to find the plant manager, could not find
him. . . . Meanwhile two more horses fell down in the alleyway. The first was the second horse in line to the knock-
box. It had fallen forward and the horse behind it began
to walk on top of it as the downed horse struggled to get
up. The second horse to fall was the fourth horse in line. It
had flipped over backwards due to the overcrowding and
was subsequently trapped and trampled by the fifth and
sixth horses in line in their excitement. . . .*

And in this statement taken from records in Cook County,
Illinois, a former slaughterhouse employee testified to the
following:

*In July 1991, they were unloading one of the double-deck-
er trucks. A horse got his leg caught in the side of the truck
so the driver pulled the rig up and the horse's leg popped
off. The horse was still living, and it was shaking. [Anoth-
er employee] popped it on the head and we hung it up and
split it open. . . . Sometimes we would kill near 390, 370
a day. Each double-decker might have up to 100 on it. We
would pull off the dead ones with chains. Ones that were
down on the truck, we would drag them off with chains
and maybe put them in a pen or we might drag them*

with an automatic chain to the knockbox. Sometimes we
would use an electric shocker to make them stand. To get
them to the knockbox, you have to shock them . . . some-
times run them up the [anus] with the shocker. . . . When
we killed a pregnant mare, we would take the guts out
and I would take the bag out and open it and cut the cord
and put it in the trash and sometimes the baby would still
be living, and its heart would be beating, but we would
put it in the trashcan.

I'd found my way to New Holland with a horse rescue
worker I'll call Pat. Like many people who start up rescues,
Pat was a lifelong rider and horse owner before opening her
rescue in 2008. When I first visited her on a cold winter
afternoon several weeks before the auction, I was led into a
paddock of ex-racehorses rescued from nearby tracks. While
we walked, Pat recounted for me the injuries that ended
the horses' careers and commented on the "bottom-dweller
trainers who would've sold them to the meat man" and the
"good trainers who call rescues to come take them." The
horses gravitated toward her, while chickens poked about
and ran under the horses' legs of gold and a Labrador puppy
jumped up to kiss the horses' long sculpted faces. "These
are Thoroughbreds?" I asked, surprised by their calmness.
"They're here for a few weeks or so, they settle in," she told
me, while leaning into the horses' bellies and cooing to
them. "Isn't that right?"

Pat was willing to take me to New Holland—driving us
north for three hours in her 100,000-plus-mileage truck,
her old trailer trailing behind us. "I need a new trailer, a new
truck, fences. Everything. But it works out, somehow. It just
does," she said after jump-starting the truck that morning as
the sun rose and the fog settled into the foothills and roost-

ers called in the background. We were heading to Pennsylvania to meet a man named Frank, who runs an auction in New Jersey.

"Frank is a kill buyer, plain and simple," says Anne Russek, a former Thoroughbred racehorse trainer who trained out of Monmouth Park Racetrack in New Jersey and who worked with HBO producers on an episode of Bryant Gumbel's *Real Sports* that aired on May 12, 2008, titled "Hidden Horses." The segment was an exposé that followed the path of a four-year-old Thoroughbred bay filly named No Day Off, who raced for the last time at Mountaineer Park Racetrack in West Virginia on April 12, 2008—just one month before the program aired. *When a Thoroughbred racehorse reaches the end of its career or is simply no longer profitable on the track, said the HBO trailer, it is often taken directly to auction and sold for meat.*

"Frank wants to work with the rescues," says Pat. "But when he has a full load of horses, he will ship them to Canada." Pat implies, as we talk in the truck about meeting with Frank, that he has of late softened a bit. When finally I glimpse him at the auction sitting not far from us on a row of bleachers, I notice that he is older than the other KBs; he has white hair, a wide face, blue eyes, and a heather-brown, zip-up cardigan that gives him a rather grandfatherly look. Later in the day, after Frank has assisted Pat with rescuing a small pony that her daughter might like, the first thing he says to me when he learns I am writing about auctions, racing, and slaughter is: "I have an excellent attorney."

The purpose of meeting Frank at New Holland was to pick up two Thoroughbred mares, former racehorses. Thoroughbred racehorses are not supposed to end up at horse auctions, nor are they to be disposed of directly off the track with the KBs in what is euphemistically referred to as "stable to table in seven days."

"I've been involved in the Thoroughbred industry for thirty-eight years," says Russek, who is now chairperson of the Thoroughbred Celebration Horse Show series, which exclusively features off-the-track Thoroughbreds. "As much as I was involved, I never realized how many Thoroughbreds were going to slaughter. It was a secret. Everybody's dirty secret. You have to show so much identification to get onto the backstretch of a racetrack, where the horses are kept, but you show nothing to get a horse off the track. When I started working on this issue I couldn't have been more surprised by the denial. Every track said, 'It's not happening at our track.' It became very apparent to me what was happening. For instance, at a track like Belmont, where it wasn't happening so much—but then a horse loses and goes to a lower-level track and the horse starts going down. They end up at Mountaineer Park, at Charlestown, at Beulah Park, Penn National. Those are where the East Coast horses end up."

Some racetracks profess that their horses do not end up at auctions or in slaughterhouses because the tracks have instituted zero-tolerance policies for such behavior from trainers and owners. But the reality, explains Monique Koehler, founder of the Thoroughbred Retirement Foundation, is a "Thoroughbred industry made up largely of owners with only modest resources and current economics that dictate that among all owners, no matter how responsible and well-intended, only a relatively few are capable of maintaining even a single Thoroughbred once it is unable to earn its keep on the track."

Though it would not be impossible to list the policies of the nearly one hundred racetracks in the U.S., consider it safe to say that there are a good number of tracks with ostensible zero-tolerance, or "no kill," policies. These "no kill" tracks attempt to clear away their injured and their low earners through more acceptable channels—retirement, retraining and adoption, or rescue; all three options are carried out by various high- and low-budget rescue groups. One inventive effort at the Finger Lakes Racetrack involves a transition barn of sorts, called the Purple Haze Center, where horses no longer able to race are retrained and stabled on the grounds of the track until they are adopted. It is the first Thoroughbred track in the country to have an in-house adoption program that is run collaboratively between track management and horsemen. And some tracks, such as Suffolk Downs in East Boston, are connected to CANTER (the Communication Alliance to Network Thoroughbred Ex-Racehorses), a group that works with trainers to identify racehorses who need homes and lists available horses on their website.

But not all horsemen take advantage of groups like CANTER or other rescue options and, apparently, resort instead to unscrupulous practices. Russek describes a place not far from New Holland that is run by a Mennonite man. "I went there hoping to establish a relationship with him," she explained. "He told me dealers bring horses from the track saying they *must* go to slaughter because trainers don't want it known what they're doing." In other words, a dead horse is harder to trace than a horse that ends up at auction when it's not supposed to.

Take the story of Twilight Overture, a gelding who came from Thistledown, "which is a 'no-kill' track," says Nena Winand. One of the rescues alerted Thistledown's general manager that the horse had been purchased by a kill buyer at the Sugarcreek Auction in Ohio. At the request of the manager, the rescue called the KB, who, surprisingly, turned his double-decker around and returned Twilight Overture to Sugarcreek for the rescue. Thistledown and Winand paid the KB $850 for the racehorse. "I renamed him Next Stop: Mars," says Winand. "Why? Because if you look at his record, he was in training from track to track to track. What does he think of his life? He was shipped every two weeks somewhere. Then he's on a double-decker to get his head bashed in. He's big, extremely athletic. His story epitomizes that slaughter is a convenient disposal system. This horse is very usable. There's no limit to what he can do; he's not bad-minded. It's default; it's convenient. That's why it's happening. Why would a trainer kill this horse, my horse? Because they want the $300 bucks they get for him from the kill buyer."

"Zero-tolerance at the tracks? Yeah, right. There's no enforcement," says Pat, when two weeks after our trip to New Holland I arrive at her rescue and find her all in a flurry trying to raise $1,500 to rescue three Thoroughbreds from Mountaineer Park. "The trainer wants $300 each or she's letting the meat man take them. And I need $200 each just to get them here. And I need it *now*." She scampers from the field to a stall to the computer to check in with contacts about the amount of money being raised to rescue the Thoroughbreds. "Everyone wants me to take two of them; you know, I just got those others. I don't have enough money to do it." Pat sighs, slipping in and out of various website forums and boards where people from across the country shoot messages back and forth. This is their battle—to save horses—and the computer is both their weapon and their battlefield. Pat pulls up photos of two of the Mountaineer Park horses in immediate need. One is a chestnut named Nitro, the other a black horse named I Gotta Go. Seeing their photos makes them real; and I am reminded that, as another Triple Crown season winds down—that time of year when Americans watch the fastest of the fast run their million-dollar races—thousands of the lesser-known Thoroughbreds, like Nitro and I Gotta Go, await their fate, having not only never made it to national television, but potentially never making it out of racing alive.

All of this sheds light on—but in the end proves nothing about—how a tall, slender, dapple-gray Thoroughbred gelding that had raced at Suffolk Downs in Boston and at Tampa Downs in Florida ended up at New Holland the morning I was there, still wearing his racing plates and standing quietly in front of me, roped to a post against a concrete wall. He already had been claimed by a KB, whom Pat would have to find and then pay more than he had paid for the gelding if she wanted to take the horse home. About a month later, I will call this kill buyer to inquire about the dapple-gray gelding. Where had the horse come from? Who'd shipped him? The KB will inform me, rather politely at first, that he is on the road with the rig and cannot give me any phone numbers. As I ask again about the journey of the dapple-gray, I picture this KB standing ringside at the auction, closest to the horses entering, along with the other KBs, all Caucasian, most in their midforties, wearing baseball caps, slouchy jackets like high-school football players, jeans, and colorful studded leather belts. Soon enough he tires of my questions.

"Who the fuck are you? Are you the horse's owner?" he rages.

"No," I answer.

"Then why the fuck are you poking your fucking nose into this?"

Of the two Thoroughbred mares we'd planned on retrieving from Frank at the auction, one was pregnant, due imminently, so Pat had spent the weekend building a foaling stall for the mare. When I called on Sunday morning to confirm our arrangements, Pat was hammering nails into plywood with a retired neighbor who volunteers. Later that afternoon, though, Pat called back to say that the pregnant mare had been inadvertently sent off on the slaughter truck a few days earlier. It was not clear how this had happened. Despite the fact that it's against regulations, she nonetheless had been dispatched on the long trip to Canada.

Probably, said Pat, she was already dead.

At the auction, Pat leaves the bleachers frequently to track down Thoroughbreds, and while she is away, quite a few of them stream in and out of the noisy bidding ring, along with other breeds, too many to list, all in and out so fast it is hard to keep track of the numbers and prices. All of the following, which is in no way a complete list, were taken by the kill buyers:

  – Thoroughbred bay gelding: $310
  – Thoroughbred chestnut gelding: $325
  – Palomino gelding, whipped several times by rider: $450
  – Two Thoroughbred geldings, lost track of price
  – Thoroughbred gelding, no price that I can hear, exits early
  – Standardbred mare, leaves the ring early. On her way out, Mennonite boys whip her repeatedly in the face. Russek will tell me later that some of the Amish and Mennonite can be "truly heartless" in the way they treat their horses, an observation that is, in all but the same words, repeated by a horse rescue worker who reported her experience at an Indiana auction on the Grateful Acres website: "The kill pen is full of Belgian draft horses, the powerful, living machinery of Amish farms. . . . [T]he Belgians in this pen are grievously and horrifyingly injured. They have been worked until they literally cannot stand any longer. . . . No matter that the animal has slaved . . . for any number of years, no matter that his swollen, oozing knee is collapsing at every forced step. Just as a broken plow would be sold to the junk man for the metal, these broken animals are sold to the kill-man for meat."

  – Thoroughbred / Quarter Horse cross: $125
  – Farm horse sold "as is" leaves ring early

– Paso Fino gelding, eleven years old, brown with white
face: $160
    – Brown and white Paint pony: $250
    – Paint gelding: $360
After two hours it becomes increasingly difficult to watch,
so I walk with Pat back into the barns to be with the horses,
though the decision to be with the animals suddenly feels
worse than staying in the bleachers. Standing so close to so
many of them, looking into their faces, rubbing their bodies,
listening to them eat hay, watching them watch us, I realize
the emotional blackmail of the moment. There is the wish
to save them all, knowing full well no one can, and that by
tonight many of them will be heading to Canada, or to feed-
lots to be fattened up for a slaughterhouse in Canada. To the
extent that one can, Pat has crossed this threshold, and her
time in the barn is more goal-directed: She weaves through
the lines of animals to find the Thoroughbreds. "Here's one,"
she yells out to me, while lifting the horse's upper lip and calling out the tattoo number for me to write down. Racehorses
are required to have a tattoo inside their upper lip, which
identifies the horse and links it to its registration papers. Soon
enough she is off with a list of tattoos to call in to a contact
waiting to help identify the racetracks to which the Thoroughbreds were last connected. Meanwhile, I scan the rows and
rows of horses and ponies, looking for the copper-colored
mare I'd seen earlier in the day, the one with the braided
mane and tail. Pat hurries back to say she has the dapple-gray
racehorse. The KB gave it over for $600. "It's a lot, but I'll
train him to jump," she says. "He'll make a good jumper, and
people love the dapple-grays."
    People love ponies, too, Pat had said at the beginning of
the auction. "They're always asking me for ponies." And so
more than midway through the auction she has bought, for

about $200 each, several ponies to adopt out as 4-H projects or as pony club mounts. One is a large, brown, bulldozerlike Hackney gelding she later will name Edward; another is a small gray boy just gelded and still shot up with testosterone who will be called Merry Legs; an unbroke Paint mare with one blue eye will become Maeve, or "the cause of great joy" in Gaelic. And then, finally, the gray roan Pony of the Americas (POA), who tentatively walks into the ring, scared enough that she'll barely move forward. She is led to stand near the fence by the kill buyers. Her eyes look up into the bleachers, her skin twitches when someone touches her, and the bidding begins. "Do you want that pony, Pat?" I ask.

"I don't have any money left. She's cute, though."

I raise my bidding card and so does a kill buyer. We start low, $35.

The KB raises his card for $40.

I go $45.

He goes $50; I raise for $60.

Zimmerman, the bearded Mennonite, looks up to me. I am new here, and I sense at that moment he knows it. He raises the bidding by $20.

KB agrees to $80. I go to $90. KB takes $95.

The auctioneer calls out $100. Zimmerman's dark eyes stare straight to mine. Once we get to $100 the price could keep climbing, and I am unsure what I can do; at the same time, I look at the POA. As much noise as there is around me—the old couple bickering, kids playing and laughing—it suddenly seems as if there is no sound, and I feel like the student in the classroom who everyone's looking at because I've been asked to answer a question I don't have an answer for.

I raise for $100.

Zimmerman looks at the KB. There is a pause. But the KB does not bid. It is over, suddenly, in a matter of seconds. "One hundred dollars for number 730-1," the auctioneer calls out.

I climb the stairs to the New Holland Auction office to pay for the pony I later will name Bridget and give to Pat; and I think how often I've blown a hundred dollars on a meaningless trip to Target. The cashier gives me the name and number of the person who unloaded Bridget at the auction because I request it. I am still naïve at this point and I assume her owners brought her here. I want to call them later to ask about their pony and tell them I have her now. That she is safe. "Charlie, here," the voice answers, when a few days later I call. "I don't know nothin' 'bout her, ma'am," the man says. "Bought her cheap at the Hickory Auction. I sell tack there and someone's sellin' her. So I take her. I bought her on Sunday and took her to New Holland on Monday. Ain't gonna lie to ya ma'am, don't know nothin' 'bout her. I buy cheap horses and resell 'em. That's what I do."

Down on the auction floor, Pat is gathering up Bridget to put her in the pen with Edward, Maeve, Merry Legs, and the dapple-gray Thoroughbred. Not long after we will meet up with Frank and transfer the mare he brought down from New Jersey. In the afternoon, when the auction is over and we are loading the horses and ponies onto Pat's trailer, around the corner will come the thin copper-colored mare with the long flaxen braids. The bones of her skinny shoulders and hips poke up from her body when she walks. She is led by a KB.

He instructs her onto his trailer. She does not move. He yanks hard on her lead rope. As thin and weak as she is, she jumps back from the trailer, her long braided mane flopping against her neck. He yells at her, harsh and fast and low, and whips her over and over in the face and on her shoulders and belly. She jumps up and throws herself against the inside wall of the trailer.

He shoves her into the horses already on the rig and they

all jostle together, colliding, biting, and agitating one another. As the dust floats up and is set aglow by the afternoon sunlight streaming into the trailer, the mare stumbles. Finally, she finds a place by the window and gazes out.

(2010)

BRIAN DOYLE

THE CREATURE BEYOND THE MOUNTAINS

Wonder, curiosity, and a really big fish

THERE ARE FISH in the rivers of Cascadia that are bigger
and heavier than the biggest bears. To haul these fish out of
the Columbia River, men once used horses and oxen. These
creatures are so enormous and so protected by bony armor
that no one picks on them, so they grow to be more than a
hundred years old, maybe two hundred years old; no one
knows. Sometimes in winter they gather in immense roiling
balls in the river, maybe for heat, maybe for town meetings,
maybe for wild sex; no one knows. A ball of more than sixty
thousand of them recently rolled up against the bottom of a
dam in the Columbia, causing a nervous United States Army
Corps of Engineers to send a small submarine down to check
on the dam. They eat fish, clams, rocks, fishing reels, shoes,
snails, beer bottles, lamprey, eggs, insects, fishing lures,
cannonballs, cats, ducks, crabs, basketballs, squirrels, and
many younger members of their species; essentially they eat

whatever they want. People have fished for them using whole chickens as bait, with hooks the size of your hand. They like to follow motorboats, for reasons no one knows. As with human beings, the males wish to spawn in their early teens, but the females wait until their twenties. The females then produce epic rafts of eggs, 3 or 4 million at a time, from ovaries that can weigh more than two hundred pounds. On average three of those eggs will grow to be mature fish. Some of the fish that have been caught have been fifteen feet long and weighed fifteen hundred pounds. There are stories of fish more than twenty feet long and two thousand pounds. A fish that long would be taller than three Shaquille O'Neals and heavier than six. There is a persistent legend in southwest Washington State that somewhere in the water near Mount Saint Helens is the biggest fish of this kind that anyone has ever seen or heard about or imagined, a fish so big that when it surfaces it is occasionally mistaken for a whale, but this is the same region of the wild and wondrous world where Sasquatch is thought to most likely live, so you wonder.

The being of which we speak is *Acipenser transmontanus*, the sturgeon beyond the mountains, popularly called the white sturgeon, although it is not white, but as gray as the moist lands in which it lives, the temperate rainforest west of the Pacific mountains and east of the not-very-pacific ocean. From northern Mexico to southern Alaska it cruises the nether reaches of rivers, battling only the sea lions that in recent years have taken up residence in the coastal rivers of the West to dine on salmon and young sturgeon, but I am sure there will come a day when I will pick up my newspaper and read about a precipitous decline in sea lion pups, and I will remember that a new lion pup is not much bigger than a chicken or a cat or a basketball. Taking the long view, you have to admire the individual sturgeon, very probably adolescent males, who over the years were the first to eat such things as cats and cannonballs. Perhaps it was accidental, but perhaps not, perhaps it was a brave leap, and among the sturgeon of today there are legends of the first heroes who inhaled volleyballs and badgers. This could be.

At the Sturgeon Viewing and Interpretive Center, at the Bonneville Fish Hatchery, in Cascade Locks, Oregon, where Tanner Creek empties into the Columbia River, near the immense Bonneville Dam, there are three enormous sturgeon in a large open pond. Two of them, each about eight feet long and weighing about an eighth of a ton, have not as yet been given names by human beings. The third is Herman, the most famous sturgeon in Oregon. Herman is more than ten feet long and weighs almost five hundred pounds. No one knows how old he is. He might be ninety years old. There are references to Herman the Sturgeon in hatchery records beginning in 1925. It is thought that there have been several Hermans, some exhibited annually at the Oregon State Fair. This Herman, who is probably not the 1925 Herman, arrived at Bonneville ten years ago, a mere nine feet and four hundred pounds, then. Many thousands of people come to see Herman every year, as they visit the hatchery's spawning rooms, holding ponds, rearing ponds, and egg incubation building, all of which are for salmon and steelhead; the three sturgeon here, and the pool of massive rainbow trout, are show ponies only, sturgeon and trout not being as close to extinction as salmon and steelhead. This hatchery alone raises a million coho salmon, 8 million chinook, and 300,000 steelhead every year, for release into various Oregon rivers. There are fish everywhere at the hatchery, leaping and milling and swirling and startling visitors, and it is remarkable and piercing to see so many miracles at once, so many mysterious beings, so many

individual adventures, so much excellent flaky accompani-
ment to fine wine, and to think where they will go and what
they will see, some of them headed into the deepest thickets
of the ocean, others into the bellies of animals of every size
and shape, but pretty much every human visitor is here also
to see Herman, and I station myself in a dark corner of the
center one afternoon and view the human beings who come
to view Herman.

There are nuns. There are schoolchildren. There is a man
wearing a cat on his shoulder. There is a woman wearing not
much more than a smile. There is a woman wearing white
plastic thigh boots and a baseball jacket. There is a deputy
mayor. There is a long-haul truck driver smoking a cigar that
smells like something died in his truck. There are teenagers
holding hands. There is a man dressed head to toe in Seattle
Seahawks fan gear, including sneakers. There is a man with
a cane and a woman with a walker. There is a girl in a wheel-
chair. There are tour groups, family outings, and a man wearing tuxedo trousers and gleaming black shoes and a motorcycle gang jacket. People eat and drink and joke and curse and
smoke and spit and gape and dawdle and laugh and several
ask me, Where's Herman? I say my experience is that he will
loom into view after a while. Some people don't wait. Some
people express annoyance with the hatchery management
and the lack of organization as regards Herman's appearance.
Others mistake Herman's eight-foot-long companions for
Herman. Others wait silently for Herman to loom into view.

The most memorable viewing for me that day was a young
man with a small boy who appeared to be his son. The father
looked like he was about nineteen, with the wispy first mustache and chin-bedraggle of a teenager. The boy, wearing a red
cowboy hat, seemed to be about three years old. The father
tried to line the boy up for a photograph, tried to get the kid to

stand still until Herman loomed into view, but the boy skittered here and there like a rabbit, the father alternately wheedling and barking at him, and finally the boy stood still, but facing the wrong direction, with his nose pressed against the glass, and the father sighed and brought his camera down to his waist at exactly the moment that Herman slowly filled the window like a zeppelin. The boy leapt away from the window and his hat fell off. No one said a word. Herman kept sliding past for a long time. Finally his tail exited stage left and the boy said, awed, clear as a bell, *Holy shit, Dad.* The father didn't say anything and they stood there another couple of minutes, both of them speechless, staring at where Herman used to be, and then they walked up the stairs holding hands.

On the way home to Portland, as I kept an eye out for osprey along the banks of the Columbia, I thought of that boy's face as Herman slid endlessly past the window. It's hilarious what he said, it's a great story, I'll tell it happily for years, but what lingers now for me is his utter naked amazement. He saw ancientness up close and personal. He saw a being he never dreamed was alive on this planet, a being he never imagined, a being beyond vast, a being that rendered him speechless with awe until he could articulate a raw blunt astonishment that you have to admire for its salty honesty. He saw wonder, face to face. Maybe wonder is the way for us with animals in the years to come. Maybe wonder is the way past the last million years of combat and into the next million years of something other than combat. Maybe the look on that kid's face is the face of the future.

The woman who married me, a slight mysterious riveting being not half as tall as Herman, grabs me by the beard in the kitchen one day and says, What is *up* with you and sturgeon, why are you so fascinated with sturgeon? And I spend days afterward trying to answer these questions for myself.

Part of it is bigness. The fact that there are wild creatures bigger and heavier than cars *right there in the river, in a city of 2 million,* is astounding, and it is also astounding that everyone totally takes this for granted, whereas I would very much like to stop people in the street about this matter, and blast-text *OMG!!!,* and set up a continual river-bottom video feed in all grade schools so kids everywhere in my state will quietly mutter, *Holy shit, Dad,* and establish the website MassiveSturgeonVisitation.com, so when a creature the size of a kindergarten bus slides to the surface suddenly in front of a Cub Scout dabbing for crab in the Columbia, he, the Cub Scout, can post an alert as soon as he changes his underwear. And the bigness of sturgeon here is mysteriously stitched, for me, into the character and zest and possibility of Cascadia; there are huge things here, trees and fish and mountains and rivers and personalities and energies and ideas, and somehow the pairing of power and peace in the piscatorial is a hint of the possible in people.

Part of it is harmlessness; they don't eat us, no matter how often we eat them. Adult sturgeon do not even have teeth, having dropped their weapons after gnashing through adolescence. We have a fairly straightforward relationship with most animals: we kill the ones who eat us, and we eat the rest. Most of the ones who eat us are bigger than we are—crocodiles, tigers, sharks, bears—but there are some animals that are bigger than we are that don't eat us, and at those we gape, and grope for some other emotion beyond paranoia and palate and pet. Whales, for example. We yearn for something *with* enormous gentle animals, something more than mammalian fellowship. We want some new friendship, some sort of intimate feeling for which we don't have good words yet.

Part of it is sheer goofy wonder; I suppose to me stur-

geon are a lovely example of all the zillions of things we do
not know, for all our brilliance and inventiveness and cocki-
ness, all our seeming confidence that we run the world. Most
of what we do know is that we don't know hardly anything,
which cheers me up wonderfully. The world is still stuffed
with astonishments beyond our wildest imagining, which is
humbling, and lovely, and maybe the only way we are going to
survive ourselves and let everything else alive survive us too.

Part of it is freshwaterness. The ocean is the densest wilderness on the planet, the jungle, the unexplored deep, filled
with mysteries and monsters, mostly unmapped, the endless
blue world where human beings are unmoored; whereas the
rivers are land veins, serpentine lakes, people paths, arteries
through the muscled earth; and we are more comfortable in
general with fresh water, which we drink and in which we
bathe, than with salt, which we cannot drink and in which we
are not only uncomfortable but essentially unwelcome. Even
the biggest rivers and lakes are stories with endings, they
can be plumbed, they are the land's liquid cousins, the land
embraces them; whereas the ocean is landless, endless wilderness, its denizens often savage and terrifying. So to ponder an
enormous creature that is not terrifying, that lives in the river
I can see from my office window, that remains pretty much a
total mystery to biologists and ichthyologists and the United
States Army Corps of Engineers—this gives me hope.

I ask fisherfolk what it's like to haul up a big sturgeon from the
bottom of a river. Like dragging a refrigerator, says one man.
Like fishing for bear, says another. Like having an air condi-
tioner on the end of your line and if you give it slack it will sink
and if you pull too hard you will snap your line, so basically you
are doomed to an hour's weight lifting, at the end of which you
haul up a nightmare from the Paleozoic, says another.

They have the most subtle bite, says a man who guides
men and women to sturgeon in the mouth of the Mighty Columbia. We call it a soft bite. You're hardly aware your hook's
been taken until you set and pull and realize there's a *dinosaur*
on your line. And they're *very* fast. People don't think they
are quick because they get so big. People think they are like
manatees or whatever, but I seen them rip off fifty yards of
line in ten seconds. They *dart,* man. Something to see, a ten-
foot animal *whipping* through the water, and they jump like
tarpon, and they tail-walk especially in shallow water, and the
first time you hook a serious dinosaur and he or she decides
to light out for the territory you're . . . flabbergasted. Awed.
Fascinating animal. Very, very adaptable. They live deep, they
live shallow, they eat everything, their only enemies are sea
lions and us. What else can I tell you? They have the worst
eyesight imaginable, but they have a *very* sharp sense of smell.
One sturgeon tagged in the Columbia showed up in San Fran-
cisco Bay. Others go out in the ocean and disappear for years.
No one knows what they're doing or how far they travel. Isn't
that wild? We think we know everything science-wise but the
fact is we know about half of nothing.

People tell me sturgeon stories. A man frying oysters in a
restaurant in Portland tells me that his grandpa told him
there used to be so many sturgeon in the Columbia that you
couldn't use a net because it would for sure get broke. A biologist from Texas tells me that sturgeon evolved into their current form long before there was a hint of person in the world.
The journalist Richard Carey notes that there are stories of
sturgeon in the Volga River in Russia weighing nine thousand
pounds, which would be twenty-eight Shaquille O'Neals, and
that some sturgeon species can whistle, and that the Kootenai
Indians of Idaho used to harpoon sturgeon from canoes they

designed to be dragged by the fish until it was exhausted and could be hauled aboard or towed to shore: sturgeon surfing. An anatomist friend of mine explains that sturgeon have cousins among the bony fishes who emerge from the water and wander around on land for brief periods looking for good things to eat, and that they have other cousins who build up speed to about forty miles an hour underwater and then leap out of the water and glide for more than five hundred feet, which is seventy-one Shaquille O'Neals, and that sturgeon themselves, along with their closest cousins the paddlefish, have such extraordinarily sensitive sensory barbels—the four long whiskerlike tissues between mouth and nose that look not unlike a teenage boy's first uncertain mustache—that they may be able to discern what *kind* of cat they are about to eat. This could be.

I kept coming back to Herman. Every once in a while I would find myself thinking about him and soon I would be in the car sailing through the stunning Columbia Gorge to stand quietly in the shadowy corner of his viewing room for a while. Without fail, every time I was there someone would be startled and say something startling. It wasn't always a kid. One time a small man with a mohawk haircut said something in a language I don't know, but his tone was unmistakable and I would bet the house he said *holy shit* in Mayan or Tagalog or whatever. Another time a man knelt and prayed when Herman hove into view. Another time a young woman came in and watched Herman for a while and then whirled on me and delivered a sudden tart lecture on how it was a *sin* and a *crime* to *jail* this fellow living *being* in this ridiculous *circus*, to which I didn't reply, there being nothing to say, and she stomped off.

I went and sat by the river for a long time after that, though. She was right; Herman is in prison for the crime of

being amazing, which doesn't seem altogether fair. And for all
you can say that he's safe, and well fed, and has lots of visitors to his jail cell, and cool roommates, and a certain renown,
especially among children, still, he is confined without cause,
and chances are excellent that he would rather be in the river,
goofing on salmon and whistling at girls and eating cats and
basketballs like the other guys.

I end up at the edge of the Mighty Columbia, which is
thought to be maybe 10 million years old and which was brawl-
ing past this spot, crammed with *Acipenser transmontanus*,
long before my forebears wandered out of Africa, gaping at
the wider world. A heron lumbers over, looking like a blue
tent. In front of me the Bonneville Dam stretches forever.
Sturgeon live so long that there are certainly elders above the
dam, upriver, who were there before the first lock was built in
1938. Perhaps they are wondering when the sudden wall in
the water will dissolve. Perhaps the vast ball of sturgeon that
boiled at the base of the dam in early 2008 was not motivated
by lust or politics or sea lion revenge plots but by the itch to
communicate with loved ones behind the Wall.

I go back and watch Herman for a while and consider that
maybe his job is to be an agent of wonder. Maybe everyone
who gapes at Herman gets a sturgeon seed planted in their
dreams. Maybe Herman is the one among his clan chosen to
awaken the walk-uprights. Maybe he watches the people who
watch him and every time a child leaps back amazed Herman
silently scores another one for the good guys. Maybe he is
here to grant us humility. Maybe humility and wonder in the
right proportions lead to wisdom.

(2011)

CHRISTOPHER KETCHAM

NEW DOG IN TOWN

The coyote as city dweller, and what it means
for the country

WILD COYOTES have settled in or around every major city in
the United States, thriving as never before, and in New York
they have taken to golf. I'm told the New Yorker coyotes spend
a good deal of time near the tenth hole on the Van Cortlandt
Park Golf Course in the Bronx. They apparently like to watch
the players tee off among the Canada geese. They hunt squirrels and rabbits and wild turkeys along the edge of the forest
surrounding the course, where there are big old hardwoods
and ivy that looks like it could strangle a man—good habitat
in which to den, skulk, plan. Sometimes in summer the coyotes emerge from the steam of the woods to chew golf balls and
spit them onto the grass in disgust.

They also frequent the eighth and the ninth and the
twelfth holes, where golfers have found raccoons with broken necks, the cadavers mauled. At the tenth hole, a coyote
ran alongside a golf cart last summer, keeping pace with the
vehicle as the golfers shook their heads in wonder. "I stop the
cart, he stops," one golfer who was there told me. "I start it
up, he follows. I jump out, he jumps back. I sit down in the

cart, he comes forward. We hit for a while—we're swinging, and he's watching." Here the golfer, an animated southerner named Chris, mimes the animal, following with his head the coyote-tracked ball's trajectory up and up, along the fairway, then its long arc down. It was pleasing to Chris that coyotes like golf.

Until recently, I couldn't quite believe that coyotes were established New Yorkers. Among neophyte naturalists, it's an anomaly, a bizarrerie, something like a miracle. Coyotes, after all, are natives of the high plains and deserts two thousand miles to the west. But for anyone who takes the time to get to know coyotes, their coming to the city is a development as natural as water finding a way downhill. It is also a lesson in evolution that has gone largely unheralded. Not in pristine wilderness, but here, amid the splendor of garbage cans filthy with food, the golf carts crawling on the fairway like alien bugs, in a park full of rats and feral cats and dullard chipmunks and thin rabbits and used condoms and bums camping out and drunks pissing in the brush, a park ringed by arguably the most urbanized ingathering of *Homo sapiens* in America—here the coyote thrives. It seemed to me good news.

The coyote, unlike its closest cousin, the wolf, is a true American. The coyote's earliest relatives began evolving in the Southwest as early as 10 million years ago, with *Canis latrans* arriving roughly at the dawn of the Pleistocene era, when huge predators roamed the continent. I imagine the coyote in its prehistoric form as a thing small and weak and quiet, slinking in the shadows alongside the megafauna of American prehistory. The little dog had to deal with the appetites of cave lions, which weighed upward of six hundred pounds; the predations of the saber-toothed cat; the fury of the short-faced bear, which, at a height of fourteen feet and a weight of up to nineteen hundred pounds, was the largest bear that ever lived. It tried not to get stomped by the mastodon and the mammoth and the stag-moose and the elephant-sized ground sloth and the armored glyptodon, a turtle as big as a Volkswagen.

Then, beginning some twelve thousand years ago, the coyote got a break. In one of the great extinction events of prehistory, North America's megafauna, these giants of the continent, disappeared. What precipitated the mass extinction is unknown, and is today the stuff of much speculation. The cause might have been climate change—the retreat of the glaciers, the warming of the planet—or perhaps it was a change in weather combined with overkill from newly arrived human predators who crossed the Bering Strait, armed with the technology of spears that the megafauna were not adapted to fend off. The coyote, fighting for so long in this hard world of giants, was among the few prehistoric American mammals to survive in the new environment. Other sizable fauna soon filled the extinction vacuum. But they were foreigners. Like the spear-chucking humans, the new mammals were descendants of Asia. They are the creatures that we know now as bison, elk, moose, bighorn sheep, grizzly bear—invasives that we generally find ghettoized in our national parks.

Another invasive species that crossed from Asia was the gray wolf. Fast-forward several thousand years, and the coyote and the wolf have become mortal enemies. They have fought for space over the millennia, with the wolf claiming most of the American continent because the wolf is bigger, more aggressive, works in packs, and operates well in dense forest. Enter the white man, whose technology and avarice allowed for sweeping control over established predators. By 1900, white settlers had decimated the wolf population, which threatened their livestock and their children. This was accomplished not simply by unleashing gunpowder; the white man felled forests everywhere he went, which opened up the terrain and left no hiding place for wolves. The coyote, on the other hand, thrived in open spaces. It was adaptable as the wolf was not; it had been adapting to predation in America for 10 million years. So the coyote took over the wolf's niche as top dog.

In the wake of white settlement, the coyote was reviled for its success. That we could not appreciate the elasticity of the native dog was fitting irony for the European species of human, so terribly successful at invading the continent and adapting to it ourselves (or, rather, forcing the continent to adapt to our new and increasingly invasive presence). Along with the Indian and the bison, the coyote was—remains—the pest par excellence of the American West, to this day classified in the law books of many western states as "vermin" or "nuisance" species. Tens of millions of coyotes have been slaughtered in the U.S. since 1900; federal and state governments over the last two decades have killed an estimated 2 million of them. This figure doesn't incorporate the tens, perhaps hundreds, of thousands of coyotes each year hunted, baited, trapped, snared, and poisoned by livestock ranchers and sport hunters who kill coyotes for recreation in contest and bounty hunts. The attempt at control has cost in the range of billions of dollars—no firm number is known—and it has failed spectacularly. Biologists note that the success of the coyote amid this carnage is largely due to a survival mechanism that renders the species impervious to the gun and the trap: when large numbers of coyotes are killed in any single ecosystem, the coyotes that remain produce bigger litters. The animal compensates for slaughter, in other words, by becoming more numerous, more problematic. I can only imagine this as a kind of Darwinian laughter: *Kill more of us, and more of us will come. Perhaps to be killed. So that there will be more of us. Ha ha!*

I first heard the sound of the eastern coyote in the sprawling Catskill Mountain range, a hundred miles north of New
York City. The creatures screamed and shouted and yipped; I
thought I was hallucinating. That was eight years ago. Only
once did I get close, in October 2002, when a pack in fog
yelled in my ear on a mountaintop. No sighting of the creatures that cold night, nothing to lay my eyes on. Just the high
keening song, the crackle and whisper of my feet and theirs
on the forest floor. Thereafter I made it a point to walk in the
forest and climb the mountains at night, to listen for them,
find their sign, their scat, their kills. Eight years later, I've
found a lot of scat, many prints in mud, and no coyotes.

But the song—it hung in my head. I'd listened to coyotes
in the American West, and the song in the East was different. In the red rock of the desert, it's lone and sorrowful and
begins with a bark (*Canis latrans*, after all, means "barking
dog"). The pack sometimes—only sometimes—answers the
loner, the voices clear and vibrant, like a Greek chorus. In
the East, vocalizations never seem to open with the loner.
The song instead begins with a scream upon a scream, followed by creeches, squeaks, eeks, heeing and hawing and
ululations, dystonal and weird, that the western cousin can't
match. I could say I hear the gamelan music of Indonesia,
the off-time rhythms of Turkic Bosnia, girls screaming rape,
men losing testicles.

A few years ago, late on a summer night in 2004, I
thought I heard a lone coyote singing in the Bronx. This was
not long after the first reported New York sightings, which
already had begun increasing in frequency. If coyotes were
on the move in the city, marking terrain, naturally, I thought,
there should be communication among them. What I heard,
wandering Van Cortlandt Park on that summer night, was a
short spindrift cry, like something heard underwater, distant

and muffled and indistinct, and later I assumed it was the
work of a dog pretending at wildness while slobbering over
an owner come home. Or perhaps it didn't happen at all and I
imagined it because I'd been reading too many reports about
coyotes. In the moment, though, I believed what I wanted,
and I started howling. And waited. And howled. There was
the hush of the city, the hoodoo silence of the buildings that
surround the park, and in the silence I could hear the mur-
murs of men and women speaking in a thousand ways out of
tune with each other, and finally, when I howled one last time,
someone leaned out a window and cried, "Shut the fuck up."

From California to Maine, there are more coyotes than at any
time since records have been kept, their territorial expansion
unprecedented in speed and scope. "The coyote is the most
successful colonizing mammal in recent history," Justina Ray,
an ecologist with the Wildlife Conservation Society, tells me.
They pressed eastward across the Plains and the Midwest. They
went south into Alabama, Georgia, Florida. By the 1920s, they
had arrived in New York State, where they advanced at a mind-
boggling rate of 116 miles per month. By 1942 they were in Ver-
mont; by 1944 they were in New Hampshire; and by 1958 they
were in western Massachusetts. I recently found their tracks
like a palimpsest in the tidal flats at Cape Cod National Seashore—the messages of their movements chasing crabs—and
one homeowner on the Cape described a den in his wooded
backyard, thirty feet from his deck, where the pups stared out
from inside a tree trunk. I talked with a Connecticut woman
who welcomed a wounded coyote into her car, thinking it was a
bashed-up dog, and took it into her house only to discover the
creature going wild in her living room as it matured—want-
ing to get out. By the 1970s, coyotes were arriving in the cold
sea-country of the Canadian Atlantic Provinces, having become

fully established in New Brunswick by 1975, reaching south-western Nova Scotia by 1980, Prince Edward Island by 1983, and floating on sea ice across the Cabot Strait to the Island of Newfoundland by 1987.

That the coyote has expanded his range does not surprise biologists. What does confound is the suggestion, hotly de-bated, that the coyotes now taking over the eastern U.S. in fact represent a new subspecies of wild dog on the continent, the so-called *Canis latrans varietas*. The western coyote is a smaller creature than the eastern cousin. The westerner weighs in at perhaps thirty pounds, looking somewhat like a fat fox. The eastern coyote grows as big as sixty pounds at his heftiest. The tracks I found on Cape Cod and in the Catskill Mountains suggest a big dog indeed.

So whence the bigger muscles, the extra weight, the new song? Perhaps natural selection in the face of bigger game, or the higher snows and colder weather of places like Chicago and New York, sparked the coyote's physical flowering. Per-haps coyotes in their dominance arrived at a sexual detente with the last wolves in the East and began breeding with their old enemies, which added to the girth of the eastern coyote and also gave him his new voice. Perhaps the wolves, in this same pivotal moment, realized they were outnumbered and preserved, in a copulative leap of hopelessness, what little remained of their genetic pool. I like to think that all these factors commingled and were further complicated by the reality of dealing with the human ecosphere—the byways and hidden passages of the city, the dynamism of interaction with cars, highways, apartment buildings replete with comings and goings, the all-night bodegas, the light of streetlamps, the con-niving of rats, the surfeit of accident and possibility. I like to think the eastern coyote's build, its behavior, and, not least, its song reflect this complexity.

So the coyote runs across schoolyards in Philadelphia; he hides under a taxi on Michigan Avenue in Chicago. He is in Atlanta, and in Los Angeles, and Miami, and Washington DC. He follows into the cities our paths, our roads, our railways, our bike and hiking trails. In Seattle, a coyote ran into an elevator in a skyscraper for a ride, and another ended up in the luggage compartment of a tram at the SeaTac Airport. In Boston, biologists who radio-collared a female coyote during 2004 reported that the dog traveled freely across the towns of Revere, Medford, Somerville, and Cambridge, at one point crossing into Boston proper via a railroad line at three a.m. before bedding down in a railyard north of the Charles River. The dog, nicknamed Fog, had "little more than shrubs for her to sleep in." Stanley Gehrt, a biologist at Ohio State University who recently spent six years tracking the coyote populations of Chicago, concluded that there were at least two thousand of them living in the Windy City, and they were growing in number. Urban coyotes, Gehrt found, live longer than their country cousins, their range per pack is more compact, much like urban humans, and they hunt more often at night (very much like urban humans). Gehrt also found that coyotes howl in answer to the sirens from firehouses—calling to the sounds of men. "Originally known as ghosts of the plains, coyotes have become ghosts of the cities," Gehrt writes. "Coyotes are watching and learning from us."

I got a beer from a bodega in the Bronx and sat on a bench and thought about the ghost dog. To the American Indians, coyote is Trickster, the magician among the animals, the shadow creature, the player on the edges of human encampments. "Along the edge I am traveling, in a sacred manner," goes an old Lakota song honoring the Trickster. Sacred manner? Wile E. Coyote chasing the Roadrunner comes more readily to mind. Chuck Jones, the animator, pegged the Trickster, in his cartoon Latin, as *Eatibus anythingus*. Which is true: coyotes eat garbage, darkness, rats, air—they'd lap my beer if I let them.

The Trickster in myth appears as rotten minded as Wile E., as creepy and ill reputed, as underhanded as Bronx rats. But in the system of native myth, unlike Wile E., unlike Bronx rats, the coyote's lying and conniving and cheating is in the last act a leap of creation, bearing the new out of things that are busted down and old and not working. The cartoon hints at this: Wile E. falling off cliffs, born again from the smashed puffball of bones at the canyon bottom to try for a meal once more.

In the various coyote myths, the Trickster makes things happen by sheer pushy will and wackiness. He is a shape-shifter, blown apart, come together again. Coyote is some-times the creator of the world itself in his tumbledown acci-dental manner; sometimes he brings fire to the hominids who are freezing in the cold; sometimes he gets the smartest and most beautiful girls pregnant when dumbstruck men can't get it up to perpetuate the line; sometimes he makes sure that animals get anuses when the Creator, whoever that fool is, forgets to do so. The Trickster, in other words, is a teacher of possibilities, pointing humankind down new paths when the poor bummed-out hominids are stumped.

My own amateur coyote study in New York's Van Cortlandt Park last autumn went not so well. Day after day, I made the long trip by subway north from Brooklyn into the Bronx, my hopes up, maps out, binoculars in the backpack, notepad ready, boots laced high, a flashlight with extra batteries in case I found the creatures after dark. I got lost in the Van Cortlandt woods, scrambling near the border with Westchester. I got paranoid about muggers (who, like coyotes, never seem to show up). I got covered in mud tramping in washes looking for tracks. I got poison ivy up my leg and into my crotch.

The golfers at the Van Cortlandt golf course snickered at my efforts. "Saw more of your little friends just the other day," they'd tell me. "Haven't found any yet?" they'd laugh. "Coyotes don't do interviews," they'd tell me. They suggested I take up golf.

I took to wandering at night where I thought coyotes might be making their way into the Bronx. I imagined them arriving in Van Cortlandt Park via the Putnam Trail, a soil vein pounded smooth as glass, where I walked and walked. Or perhaps they followed the Old Croton Aqueduct Trail, the outmoded passage for the Catskill reservoir water that keeps the city alive (the Croton Aqueduct has long been supplanted by more modern piping). From the Bronx, the passage south onto the island of Manhattan is more difficult. Perhaps they cross the Harlem River, swimming the water, or, more likely, they walk the bridges at night. It is only some five miles from the tip of Manhattan to Central Park, which is the place to be if you're a coyote in Manhattan. On April Fool's Day 1999, a coyote named Lucky Pierre led reporters, helicopters, photographers, cops, and tourists in a chase across Central Park before succumbing to a tranquillizer dart. Pierre got his name because for a time he holed up in a cave across from the luxe Pierre Hotel. In the winter of 2004, a coyote was seen bounding among the ice floes on frozen Rockaway Inlet in Queens, near the dunes of Breezy Point, twenty-five miles south of Central Park. The animal apparently had gotten across Manhattan, across the East River, either dog-paddling in the water or hiking one of the bridges to Brooklyn, and thence across that borough to the shores where Brooklyn meets Queens and the sea. Cops in boats tried to capture the creature, but he dove in the cold surf, swam to shore, and was gone.

A coyote made it across Brooklyn? Incredible. I sometimes find it hard to cross Brooklyn.

On Super Bowl Sunday 2006, on Manhattan's Upper
West Side, a coyote was found smashed at the side of a high-
way. That same year, a second coyote was captured in Central
Park. In 2008, a coyote appeared on the Bronx campus of the
Horace Mann School, the *New York Sun* reporting that it was
out for a "jog" with the students and "offered no resistance"
when animal-control officers scooped it up. On February 4,
2010, a coyote, described as "timid and skittish," stopped in
the middle of a frozen Central Park pond long enough to be
captured on film by a photographer. Three days later, a trio of
coyotes appeared out of nowhere on the Columbia University
campus in upper Manhattan, then disappeared as quickly. On
March 24, a coyote was reported inside the Holland Tunnel,
then it was sighted wandering Tribeca. "Manhattan's coyote
population continued its inexorable push southward," concluded the *New York Times*. There will of course be many
more of them, and we will welcome the romance of the wild
dogs, until we don't. The creatures will have to be hunted
and killed once they hunt and kill one too many of our domesticated foot-warmers (or, worse, the little ones in our own
domesticated breed). We like our gardens in the East, we like
our vines run amok, our tall trees in the backyard, the deer
grazing on bluegrass, the pretense of wildness; we like our
animals at home pretending at atavistic habits, but we don't
want a carcass at the door in the morning. In other words,
let's have gardens, but not nature. Herein lies the irony of the
coyote's arrival in the urban East. He does not represent wildness; he is an adaptee to the garden. Without us subjugating
the land to the ridiculous extent that we have, he wouldn't be
walking alongside us.

My guide to the parks of the Bronx was a fifty-six-year-old
New York City Parks Department wildlife biologist named

Dave Kunstler, who gives the impression that he prefers the conversation of nighthawks and tree frogs. It was October, the days growing short, and we hiked the woods until dusk, looking for coyote dens where he suspected they might be, finding none. We searched under rocks, behind boulders, in tree trunks. We ended up purloining a golf cart at the Van Cortlandt golf course to hunt them on the fairway. Kunstler didn't seem much interested in the quest. What he mostly talked about were invasive plants. Kunstler saw invasives everywhere pushing out the natives: porcelain-berry and Asiatic bittersweet and mugwort; the *Ailanthus* and the Norway maple among the tall trees; and elsewhere, whole stretches of forest swallowed in kudzu.

Many of the plants Kunstler pointed out could be classified as weeds. Coyotes, it seems to me, are also a kind of weed species. And their success is indicative of a larger problem facing the human race, the problem of weeds relentlessly encroaching, their effect the strangulation and diminishment of complex ecosystems everywhere. Weed species, writes David Quammen, "reproduce quickly, disperse widely when given a chance, tolerate a fairly broad range of habitat, take hold in strange places, succeed especially in disturbed ecosystems, and resist eradication once they're established. They are scrappers, generalists, opportunists." The coyote, exactly. Also, black rats, cockroaches, crows, kudzu, raccoons, the white-tailed deer, ragweed, Russian thistle, feral cats, feral dogs, squirrels, wild turkeys—all of them weed species, all exploding in number across the country, but especially along the suburban-urban gradient. In his essay "Planet of Weeds," Quammen singles out another spectacularly successful weed species, *Homo sapiens*, and notes that other weeds down the food chain tend to follow where human beings tread. The planet of weeds, as Quammen describes it, is an impoverished place in its abundance because it heralds the end of diversity. And it is likely our inexorable future.

Kunstler and I rode around on the cart like a pair of tin cans, driving away beautiful geese, hundreds of them fleeing on the fairway—weeds with wings. We rode and rode.

Eventually, we stopped a young man who was tending to the carts. "Sure, I seen one just yesterday."

I threw up my hands.

"They're probably watching us right now," Kunstler shrugged.

Not finding a single coyote suddenly made me depressed.

Where is Trickster? We need him. The hominids are screwing up and don't have a plan to fix things. We've got global warming and rising seas and peak oil and fish dying off and deserts spreading. We've got a planet of weeds, and we seem utterly incapable of adapting to forestall disaster. The coyote survived the great Pleistocene extinction, and may very well survive the present one, the planet's sixth great extinction, an event that has been greatly accelerated by the industrialization of *Homo sapiens* to the point that many thousands of species have disappeared in the last century alone. One wonders whether, before it is all through, *Homo sapiens* might be among the deceased. Perhaps the message that Trickster brings to us is this: *The more of us you see, the more impoverished the world will be.*

(2010)

MARY OLIVER

WASTE LAND

An Elegy

AT OUR TOWN's old burn dump, not officially used for years,
discarded peppermint and raspberries reconnected their roots
to the gravelly earth and went on growing; a couple of apple
trees blossomed and bore each year a bushel of green and
bumpy fruit. Blackberries drifted up and down the slopes;
thistles, bouncing bet, everlasting, goldenrod, wild carrot
lifted their leaves and then their flowers and then their rafts of
seeds. Honeysuckle, in uplifted waves, washed toward some
pink roses, no longer a neat and civilized hedge but a thorny
ledge, with darkness at its hem.

  Now the burn dump is no more. The old world had its
necessities; presently there are new ones, and they are not so
simply met—nor will the old parcels of land suffice. On these
few acres of land, and more, will be established the heartland
of our town's sewage, where buried pipes will converge with
the waste of our lives. What a sad hilarity! I want to talk about
flowers, but the necessity has become, for our visitor-rich
town, how to deal with the daily sewage of, it may be, sixty
thousand souls. At least that was a weekend estimate a few
years ago. They come, to this last town on the long Cape, in

good part for the very beauty that their numbers imperil. They come for fellowship, the beaches and the sun, the entertainment, the shops and restaurants. They inhabit old captains' houses turned into inns, or the condominiums ever rising along newly created streets and crowded cul-de-sacs. So, this is an elegy.

In the summers, black snakes swirled among the creamy blossoms of the honeysuckle and the pink-petaled roses. When I walked through the grass, their black faces appeared, like exotic flowers. There were almost always two of them, sometimes three. One had eyes the color of garnets. It gave no greeting, only a long, motionless gaze. And they were brave, those snakes. Occasionally when I came upon a pair sleeping in the sun, on stones or a heap of old asphalt shingles, one of them would streak toward me and fling itself against my body, before it turned and followed the other away, whipping after it into the shadows under the roses.

Soon they will be off, hunting another place to live. Which may not be so easy, for the world today is nothing if it is not sprawl, and not only within the residential areas, but the seemingly endless facilities such settlements need. And we do need them. (So, this is an elegy.)

Box turtles nested here, and painted turtles also. Out of the shallow ponds below the crest of the hill, snapping turtles crawled to lay their pale, leathery eggs. Raccoons aspire to them; many of the nests were ransacked as soon as the turtle had shuffled away. Foxes left their dainty tracks, and in summer the red-coated deer.

The toad was always here, with his gold-rimmed eyes.

And, in a certain shaded place nearby, the uncommon, cool, and gleaming bunchberry.

For years there were signs posted, prohibitions against leaving trash. In more recent years another sign designated the area a motorcycle and motorbike course. The bikes appeared most often in the afternoons; they snarled over the field, they cut ruts along the trails, they raced with a furious, uncontainable form of boy-energy and noise. I hated it, yet did not resent it. There must be a place for boys and their trappings, though surely it should not have been here, on one of the few town-owned woodlands, fresh and untrammeled except for its polluted center. Also, it joined seamlessly with the national seashore, and what young boy hunched over the handlebars of his bike could remember that invisible line? So sections of the park's shady paths also became rutted by tires and besotted by blown trash. But when space is limited for recreations of such different kinds, compatibility is given improbable tasks.

As for the trash, which gathered in spite of the signs, it did what trash does and ever will do; it lay there, and did not grow thin or fade or even, much of it, rot. Old stoves were predominant. And dozens of tires, lining the bike track, the standing water within them breeding uncountable numbers of mosquitoes.

And yet, at certain hours, in the absence of boys and their bikes, I could walk here and see birds I found nowhere else: the indigo bunting, for example, and the black-billed cuckoo. And their more findable associates: goldfinches, catbirds, the brown thrasher, the yellowthroat, palm warblers, the grosbeak. The ruby-throated hummingbird nested here, but even now I will not tell you in precisely what tree. It was a secret to be kept then, so why not keep it still, now that the birds and the tree itself have vanished? And there were daisies, and butter-and-eggs, and milkweed with its mauve pendants, and black-eyed Susans. There were rugosas, white and red. In the summer light they shot upward, heavy with buds and pleated, glossy leaves. Then sagged under their own sweet weight.

But this is an elegy. Now there are buildings to take care of this new and important work. A brick building, neat and Cape Cod enough that it could almost be a bank! And behind it a huge, circular cement construction—I cannot call it a building—round and thick-walled: not built for beauty, and not yet finished. Piles of pipes are everywhere. The blackberries that climbed up and down the hill, the goldenrod, the honeysuckle are gone; the pink roses are gone; the fox tracks are gone.

The land itself has been capped against the poisons that have been seeping all these years into the ground, from the fires, from the unknown elements cast away: oils and paints and car batteries and a hundred offensive substances more. And, imagine!, for what unaware years I picked the blackberries and the raspberries, and thought them sweet and fine—thought them good fortune. And found, on the rubbled hillsides, strange shapes of old jars, glass bent and reshaped by the flames. Nuggets of deep blue from medicine containers; once a glass airplane that originally held candy, with a chip missing from one wing.

But, this is an elegy. A part of the book of not-wanting-to-let-go. And, go it must; and go it has. The pink roses and the toad with gold-rimmed eyes. The young boys on bikes who in fact are men now. Even the tires are gone. The town government has made its not unreasonable decision. We cannot continue with failing cesspools; we cannot condone seepage into the water supply, or into the blue harbor that lies along the town's frontage. And, we are so many.

In May the moccasin flowers blossomed, even in this thin soil, extravagantly. They stood in gatherings of six or seven, like small choirs getting ready to sing. Very rarely, one flower would rise pure white.

I do not like what has happened. I do not hold the loss lightly. I wish to be reasonable; I know I must be amenable to what is necessary. But—such few choices! I apologize to the hummingbird. I hope the snakes have found a new home. I hope the new system works. I am glad that I have a good memory; I will not forget the dainty tracks of the fox, or the goldfinches, or the everlasting. I think I know what our manifest, tree-filled, creature-lively world is—our garden and our pasture and our recreation. Also it is our schoolhouse, courthouse, church, graveyard, and the soft breath of eternity.

I walk in the world to love it. Only one question, really, frightens me. I wonder why, in all the years I walked in the old burn dump—this waste place, this secret garden—I never met another soul there, who had come forth for a like reason.

(2003)

CRAIG CHILDS

SEEING DEER

An autumnal elegy

OCTOBER'S HUNTERS have gone into the mountains. Smoke from their campfires rises from wild, green canyons. This time of year, the deer descend into low country for the coming winter, departing with the first frost, the first light snow, the first booming echoes of rifles. They come down to drift and mingle in fields below the mountains, touching damp noses to each other, neighbors from distant valleys meeting in cool evening light.

Younger bucks stay together, stepping like teenagers abreast of one another, their parades of antlers nearly touching, but not. They cannot hide their lives in the open country of their autumn range. Everything they do is visible. When I spy older bucks alone, I think them senile, perhaps, dominance having gotten to them so they can hardly look at anything but the spread of their own territory. They seem paranoid and irritable, nipping at the hinds of does to get them out of the way, while young bucks watch with anticipation.

Autumn is the season of rut. Fights break out. One at a time young males with four fresh points on their antlers break away to challenge old ones who wear six or even eight points.

They provoke each other over fields of females. They posture and snort. They wrestle each other to the ground with their antlers. I saw them do this one moonless October night. I was driving south when two bucks swung into my headlights. With heads butted nearly to the ground, they locked antlers, dragging and shoving one another into the middle of the road. Hooves coughed up dust. They did not even glance at my sudden headlights as I stepped on the brakes. My little boy was in the back seat and I told him to look, that buck deer were fighting. He leaned his body as far as he could out of his car seat and asked why they were doing this. I told him it is a season called autumn, or fall. Deer fight this time of year to see who is stronger. Sons try to topple their fathers. My boy stared over my shoulder, astonished.

The two animals moved swiftly, throwing each other this way and that, catapulting across the road and out of my headlights. They continued into the black of night where they went on in my imagination, tearing and scrapping like gods through the rest of time.

Near winter, on crisp evenings, you see events like this. The deer, having made their lives public, sleep, eat, fight, and copulate below wrinkled folds of mountains. They come in such numbers that many are killed by cars, their carcasses leaving streaks of blood and muscle across the road. Some lie in ditches, bundles of legs. Others are left cocked in the middle of the road where a driver got out to inspect a broken, bloodied headlight and then got back in to drive away, steering around the warm, dead animal. The eyes of these deer look like tarnished glass, and in the morning their curved milky surfaces are touched by frost.

In twenty years of driving back roads I've never hit a deer. There were close scrapes, of course, clipping off a bit of tail-

hair with my door handle or nicking a dewclaw, but I never hit
a deer dead-on. My mother hit one; my wife. Everyone I knew
hit a deer, and some did it more than once. I thought maybe
I was blessed. Deer medicine. Ungulate fortune. I talked to
them through my windshield when I saw them approaching
the side of the road, telling them to stop, directing them left
or right with a hand raised off the steering wheel. Each time,
these unseen gestures worked, the deer avoided me, and I
began thinking myself invincible, a deer whisperer.

My luck ended with a young buck. It jumped a fence in
the face of a radiant, harvest-light sunset. I pumped hard into
the brakes and urgently muttered, *Stop.*

The buck did not stop. I jammed the brakes all the way
down and my truck skidded, fishtailing across gravel. The
animal was square in the grill plate when I saw it shoot into
the air. It was making its escape, all of its life given to a single, fleeing bound, muscles coiled into flight. It was so close I
thought its hooves would clatter across my hood. In that half
second I felt a gust of relief, thinking we were going to barely
graze past each other, another near hit.

Then came a dark thud. Four slender, black hooves spun
in the air and my truck came to a halt. Copper-colored dust
welled up around the road. My hands were gripped tight to
the steering wheel. I looked over the hood, where the deer
snapped back to its feet and dove from the road, sailing over
barbed-wire fence into another field. Again I felt relief, and let
out a nerve-wracked sigh. *The deer will be fine.*

But once the deer reached the other side of the fence it
fell into a weakened hobble. I closed my mouth and drew
my lips tightly together. About forty feet from the road it
dropped into grass up to its shoulders. My heart sank. From
the way the buck fell to the ground I could see how its body
was wrecked, internal organs skewered by broken bones.

Adrenaline had been its last defense, just enough to get itself out of the road.

From inside the truck I saw that the buck's breathing was labored, almost convulsive. I opened the door and stepped out. In a week, I thought, that place in the grass will be occupied by ravens. Magpies will land on the carcass looking like jesters in their black and white feathers, their long tails. The buck will become bones by winter, ribs splintered by coyotes, antlers sticking out of snow.

I felt awkward, not sure if I should get back in and drive away or if a formal apology was needed. Should I hop the fence and slowly walk across the field, where I would plant my hands on the buck's heaving heart, where I would explain that I had been in a hurry to get to town and the sunset was so bright in my eyes? The buck looked back toward me. The way he held up his head, alert, seemed to tell me not to bring my apologies across the field. He would simply have to rally again, taking his last bit of life to reach another place where he could die in peace.

I did not cross the fence. I stood and watched the buck work his breath in and out.

A small herd of does crossed nearby. One separated from the others to stand beside the fallen buck. She lowered her snout and nearly touched her black nose to his side. Then she lifted her head and stood still for a long time, the buck's antlers raised beside her. Both of them were preserved by sunset light, everything about their living and dying naked in this autumn field. It was too private to watch. I got back in the truck and drove away.

(2007)

AMY LEACH

RADICAL BEARS IN THE FOREST DELICIOUS

The elusive, unwavering panda

THERE ONCE WAS a king of Babylon who was too proud, so he was given the mind of an animal and put out to pasture. For seven years he roamed the fields on all fours and munched on grass, after which period he was allowed to return to his palace and rich robes of purple, his barley beer and skewered locusts and royal hairdresser who gave him back his dignified ringlets. (Along with an animal's mind he had been given the animals' hairstylist.) It is not specified which animal's mind Nebuchadnezzar received, but from his glad return to civilization and fine cuisine we can infer that it was not the mind of a panda bear. If he had had a panda's mind for seven years, in the end he would have rejected the restitution of his kingdom; he would have somersaulted away, to continue leading a free, elusive, unfollowed life.

Having followers is an honor pandas dream not of. There is no tragopan so trustworthy, no bush pig so dependable that they would want it tagging along. Pandas even head away from pandas, like the stars in the universe, spreading farther and farther apart (you can never be too far away to say goodbye)— except their territory is neither infinite nor expanding, and in order to deliver more panda bears into existence, they can't just scatter into particles at the end. Pandas come together every two years or so; marriage isn't always marriage of the mind.

Maybe if they had been given a choice they would have picked a less conspicuous coat, one to better correspond with their reclusive spirits. Admirers can be secret admirers and afflictions can be secret afflictions but pandas cannot be secret pandas, since they contrast dramatically with green ferns, gray rocks, pink rhododendrons, and their own bellies and ears and legs. They are showy bears, sensationally visible, which might actually be an advantage for a solitary species: the easier to avoid you, my dear. Camouflaged animals must always be bumping into each other.

What does the animal do all day who is not engaged in society, its duties and pleasures and ferments? There may be some wedging in trees, some gazing into the mist, some fiddle-faddle. Sometimes the panda breaks an icicle off a branch and tosses it into the air over and over till it melts. Sometimes, trotting pigeon-toed across a hillside, he trips, then rolls, because he is round; having enjoyed that, he climbs back up and rolls back down. He might pick wild irises or crocuses and recline among the fern fronds to eat them, or lounge underneath a weeping willow, munching on the little leaflets that dangle into his mouth.

Mostly what pandas do with their time is eat bamboo. Bamboo, that sturdy wooden grass, comprises as much as 99 percent of their diet, and they eat it for up to fourteen hours a day. They have to consume it constantly since they are only assimilating about 20 percent. Their penitential diet is a mystery; pandas are like celery saints—everyone else is convivially dining on stuffed eggs, truffled fingerlings, little pies, and oranges, enjoying the tableside crooners, while out behind a bush sits a celery saint with his basket of celery, crunch crunch crunch. Eat enough pies and you can put aside the desire for food and pursue something else, such as a cowhand. Rare is the romance of the celery extremist.

With their carnivorous anatomy and herbivorous behavior, it is as if pandas are pledged to an ancient covenant—as if they used to be bon vivants like other bears, blood and berry juice staining their muzzles, slugabeds all winter, until one day they fell into a trance and received a deep message: "You are standing, pandas, on the very borders of the eternal world, but you have become charmed with infatuating food; the subtle poison of sensuality courses through your veins. You must disregard custom and the strong clamoring of appetite and passion. It will take, at times, every particle of willpower you possess; but give yourselves wholly to a bamboo diet, and guided by firm, unspotted principle your lives will become pure and noble." Thus was formed that radical sect of bears, the Bambooists. Modern-day Bambooists show a remarkable resistance to temptation: A stream runs by, serving up fresh fish, and what does the panda do? Wades across, to get to a stiff thicket of bamboo on the opposite side.

But willpower might not entirely account for such abstemiousness anymore. Bamboo is not power food, and the bear who eats it is not a power bear, and swiping fish from the river takes energy, as does sleeping all winter. If you're going to sleep for seven months you need to eat your hickory nuts, your ungulates, your honey. Bambooists have to stay awake all winter to eat bamboo—incidentally witnessing the sapphirine sparkles of snow falling from a branch, the cliffs draped with icy fringes, the white snow powdering the green bamboo leaves. (Could any dream compare with winter?)

What does a panda know, who studies just a few cloudy-mountain miles of the world? From her experience she must know about fallibility. Icicles melt, flowers fail, intangibly small babies grow tangible and autonomous, and one day when you come back from foraging to collect yours from the tree fork where you left him, he is gone. Mushrooms, moon-light, everything is ephemeral, with one exception: bamboo. Bamboo never fails, bamboo is eternal, evergreen, green in the orange season, green in the white season, green in the green season, poking up sweet little shoots into the spring rain. Blessed is the bear that trusteth in bamboo.

For lucky pandas it is true, bamboo never fails. Bamboo can be eternal for a hundred years, which is four times as eternal as panda bears; but there is in the character of bamboo a devastating defect. Most grasses stagger their dying, piece by piece, like an orchestra—though an oboist goes down, the collective life carries on. The trouble with bamboo is that it crashes all at once: after a century of continuous availability the entire thicket flowers together, dies together, and like a dead orchestra it can take twenty years to get back on its feet.

At this point an animal might wise up and become a Whateverist. With so many edibles in the world why consume, almost exclusively, a miserably nutritious, erratically fallible one? It's not as if bamboo is pleasant to eat, like horsebeans; bamboo splinters poke and scratch the swallower all the way down. That old covenant was arbitrary and perverse; bamboo is a silly staple; specialism is folly. Consider pragmatists—when the linguini runs out, a pragmatist will eat the center-piece, and when that is done he will eat the tablecloth. As pragmatists have no principles their numbers are myriad.

But pandas betrayed by bamboo go looking for bamboo. For there is such a thing as specialized hunger, being hungry for one thing—similar to specialized loneliness. Sometimes they don't have to travel far; pandas eat several kinds of bamboo, and even though arrow bamboo collapses, there might be umbrella bamboo growing nearby. Sometimes they have to go farther afield, and sometimes they travel in pitiful directions—would you know which way to go to find a hotbed of celery?—until their coats don't fit very well anymore. Vagrancy used to be easier on the animals, because there used to be more forest. Even if an expedition wasn't efficient, it was foresty all the way, just as the journey from earth to heaven is milky all the way. Now, between patches of forest, there are villages and gravel mines, steep cornfields, dance tents, frightened people waving blankets, mushroomers, other things to avoid.

People have tried to help pandas become pragmatists, to see sense, to switch to alternatives during a bamboo strangulation. And in captivity they comply—they eat the yams and bananas and fish set before them. But compliance is not conversion. When they are set free, pandas return to their ruinous fidelity to bamboo, shuffling past opportunity—for on the far side of that hill might be The Forest Delicious, where they can lie back in the million-column sanctuary, a bamboo cane in each forefoot, crunching on the one and then the other, munching on flappy bundles of leaves. There are fewer than twenty-five hundred free pandas left and they're all in the same boat, made of bamboo. When it goes down they go down with it, into dark water, and they won't switch to another boat, not for all the tea in China. Pandas have their own wisdom, unaccountable and unamendable, whose roots shoot down deeper than we can penetrate, and if they mind anyone at all it is someone more elusive than man.

(2012)

CONTRIBUTORS

Craig Childs writes about our relationship with animals, time, and landscape; archaeological thievery; ancient cultures; the nature of wild rivers; and what it's like to wander around in the driest places on earth. He has written more than a dozen highly acclaimed books and is a commentator for NPR's *Morning Edition*. His work has appeared in the *New York Times, Outside, The Sun*, and in *High Country News*, where he is a contributing editor. His latest book, *Apocalyptic Planet*, won the Sigurd Olson Nature Writing award as well as the Orion Book Award. Craig lives in Western Colorado with his wife and two young sons.

Lisa Couturier is the author of the book *The Hopes of Snakes and Other Tales From the Urban Landscape*. She received a 2012 Pushcart Prize for her essay "Dark Horse" and is cited as a notable essayist in *Best American Essays* 2006 and 2011. She lives in Montgomery County Maryland's Agricultural Reserve with her family and six horses. She is currently at work on a memoir.

Brian Doyle is a shambling shuffling muttering male creature who edits *Portland Magazine* at the University of Portland— "the best spiritual magazine in America," says Annie Dillard. He is the author of many books, among them the sprawling Oregon novel *Mink River* and the essay collection *The Thorny Grace of It*.

David Gessner is the author of eight books, and is at work on a ninth, *Properly Wild*, about following the ghosts of Wallace Stegner and Edward Abbey around the American West. *The*

Tarball Chronicles, his story of the BP oil spill, won the 2012 Reed Award for Best Book on the Southern Environment and the Association for Study of Literature and the Environment's award for best book of creative writing in 2011 and 2012. He is a Professor at the University of North Carolina at Wilmington, where he founded the award-winning literary journal of place, *Ecotone*. He can also be found at Bill and Dave's Cocktail Hour, a website he created with the writer Bill Roorbach.

Kathleen Jamie was born in the west of Scotland in 1962. One of the UK's foremost poets, her selected poems *Waterlight* was published in the U.S. by Graywolf. A new collection, *The Overhaul*, won the 2012 Costa Poetry Prize. Kathleen Jamie also writes nonfiction, including the highly regarded *Findings* and, recently, *Sightlines*, published in the U.S. by The Experiment Press. She is Chair of Poetry at Stirling University, and she lives with her family in Fife.

Christopher Ketcham, a contributing editor at *Harper's*, still spends a week or two each year looking for coyotes in his native New York City.

Amy Leach is the author of *Things That Are*, published by Milkweed Editions. She holds an MFA in creative nonfiction from the University of Iowa, and her work has appeared in *Best American Essays, A Public Space*, and *The Gettysburg Review*, among other journals. She has been recognized with the Whiting Writers' Award and a Rona Jaffe Foundation Award and lives in Montana.

J.B. MacKinnon is the author or coauthor of four books of nonfiction, including *The 100-Mile Diet* (with Alisa Smith) and, most recently, *The Once and Future World*. MacKinnon also works in the field of interactive documentaries. He was the writer for *Bear 71*, which was named 2012 Site of the Year at the international Favourite Website Awards. He was also text editor for *Welcome to Pine Point*, which won two Webby Awards, and is working with the Canadian Broadcasting Corporation on an interactive ebook about the Canadian wilderness. As a journalist, MacKinnon has won more than a dozen national and international awards.

Sy Montgomery—while researching articles, films, and her many books—has been chased by an angry silverback gorilla in Zaire, ridden on camels in the Gobi, swum with pink dolphins in the Amazon, and gone scuba diving with octopuses. Her work with man-eating tigers, the subject of her book *Spell of the Tiger*, was made into in a National Geographic television documentary she scripted and narrated. Also for National Geographic TV, she developed and scripted *Mother Bear Man*, about Ben Kilham, who raises and releases orphaned bear cubs. She lives in New Hampshire with her husband, writer Howard Mansfield; their border collie, Sally; and six hens.

Mary Oliver has published numerous books of poetry and also collections of essays. She won the Pulitzer Prize in poetry for her book *American Primitive* (1983) and the National Book Award for her *New and Selected Poems* (1992). Her latest book is *Dog Songs*.

Pattiann Rogers has published fourteen books, most recently *Holy Heathen Rhapsody and The Grand Array: Writings on Nature, Science, and Spirit.* Rogers is the recipient of two NEA grants, a Guggenheim Fellowship, and a Lannan Literary Award in poetry. Among other awards, her poems have received five Pushcart Prizes, two appearances in *Best American Poetry*, and five appearances in *Best Spiritual Writing.* Her papers are archived in the Sowell Family Collection of Literature at Texas Tech University. She has two sons and three grandsons and lives with her husband, a retired geophysicist, in Colorado.

ABOUT ORION MAGAZINE

SINCE 1982, *Orion* has been a meeting place for people who seek a conversation about nature and culture that is rooted in beauty, imagination, and hope. Through the written word, the visual arts, and the ideas of our culture's most imaginative thinkers, *Orion* seeks to craft a vision for a better future for both people and planet.

Reader-supported and totally advertising-free, *Orion* blends scientific thinking with the arts, and the intellectual with the emotional. *Orion* has a long history of publishing the work of established writers from Wendell Berry, Terry Tempest Williams, and Barry Lopez to Rebecca Solnit, Luis Alberto Urrea, and Sandra Steingraber.

Orion is also grounded in the visual arts, publishing picture essays and art portfolios that challenge the traditional definition of "environment" and invite readers to think deeply about their place in the natural world. *Orion*'s website, www.orionmagazine.org, features multimedia web extras including slide shows and author interviews, as well as opportunities for readers to discuss *Orion* articles.

Orion is published bimonthly by The Orion Society, a nonprofit 501(c)3 organization, and is available in both print and digital editions.

Subscribe

Orion publishes six beautiful, inspiring issues per year. To get a free trial issue, purchase a subscription, or order a gift subscription, please visit www.orionmagazine.org/subscribe or call 888/254-3713.

Support

Orion depends entirely on the generous support of readers and foundations to publish the magazine and books like this one. To support *Orion*, please visit www.orionmagazine.org/donate, or send a contribution directly to *Orion* at 187 Main Street, Great Barrington, MA, 01230.

To discuss making a gift of stock or securities, or for information about how to include *Orion* in your estate plans, please call us at 888/909-6568, or send an e-mail to development@orionmagazine.org.

Shop

Head to the *Orion* website, www.orionmagazine.org, to purchase *Orion* books, organic cotton t-shirts, and other merchandise featuring the distinctive *Orion* logo. Back issues from the past thirty years are also available.

MORE BOOKS FROM ORION

ORION READERS

Orion Readers collect landmark *Orion* essays into short thematic volumes:

Change Everything Now. A selection of essays about ecological urgency.

Thirty-Year Plan: Thirty Writers on What We Need to Build a Better Future. An eloquent statement on the future of humanity.

Wonder and Other Survival Skills. A collection of thoughtful and inspirational writing on our relationship to the natural world.

Leave No Child Inside. Essays that propose a radical reconnection of children and nature through education.

Beyond Ecophobia: Reclaiming the Heart in Nature Education, by David Sobel. An expanded version of one of *Orion*'s most popular articles that speaks to those interested in nurturing in children the ability to understand and care deeply for nature from an early age.

Into the Field: A Guide to Locally Focused Learning, by Claire Walker Leslie, John Tallmadge, and Tom Wessels, with an introduction by Ann Zwinger. Curriculum ideas for teachers interested in taking their students out of doors.

Place-Based Education: Connecting Classrooms & Communities, by David Sobel. A guide for using the local community and environment as the starting place for curriculum learning, strengthening community bonds, appreciation for the natural world, and a commitment to citizen engagement.

ORION ANTHOLOGIES

Finding Home: Writing on Nature and Culture from Orion *Magazine*, edited by Peter Sauer. An anthology of the best writing from *Orion* published from 1982 to 1992.

The Future of Nature: Writing on a Human Ecology from Orion *Magazine*, selected and introduced by Barry Lopez. An anthology of the best writing from *Orion* published from 1992 to 2007.

FOR EDUCATORS

Ideal for reading groups and academic course adoption, many *Orion* books are accompanied by a downloadable teacher's guide consisting of key discussion questions. Teacher's guides can be found on the *Orion* website at www.orionmagazine .org/education.

Series design by Hans Teensma,
principal of the design studio Impress
(www.impressinc.com), which has
designed *Orion* since 1998.
The typeface is Scala, designed by Dutch
typographer Martin Majoor in 1990.
Printed by BookMobile.